THE MERMAID LEAGUE

A Memoir of courage, hope and healing in Hawaii

SARAH SPRECHER

ABOUT THE AUTHOR

Sarah Sprecher is a writer, advocate, and long-time Maui resident whose journey began with her adoption from South Korea. Her experiences have shaped a life marked by resilience, introspection, and meaningful friendships.

Over more than two decades on Maui, Sarah has actively engaged with the island's culture, bringing integrity and intention to every role—from guiding visitors through island adventures to managing her own small business. Each of these roles reflects her deep commitment to honoring the generosity of Maui's community.

Sarah passionately believes in storytelling as an essential tool for healing, self-discovery, and strengthening communities. In, The Mermaid League, she shares more than her personal story; she invites readers into an intimate space dedicated to empowering others to embrace authenticity, resilience, and mutual strength.

THE
MERMAID
league

Through shared strength and stories
The Mermaid League
hopes to transform reflection into
a connected community

To learn more visit

mermaid-league.com

CONTENTS

chapter 1

ALWAYS, I HAVE HATED BEING HUNGRY

I was abandoned in front of a restaurant in Korea when I was just a baby. Sometimes, I wonder how long I was left there---alone, unnoticed, and unwanted.

When I was finally discovered, there was only a sheet of paper next to me, which showed my date of birth and nothing more.

I spent the first year-and-a-half of my life an orphan, with only one memory: hunger. A hunger of food, a hunger for love, a hunger for connection.

I was adopted by an American couple and taken to live with them and their three young boys. When I arrived in the states, I had lice and I could not walk, talk, or stop eating.

~ 1 ~

My belly grew quickly, and my family proudly bestowed me with the nickname of little Buddha. My appetite was bottomless. Sometimes, my mother would find raisins tucked in the back of my mouth, hidden away like a squirrel with cheeks full of nuts. I was saving them just in case.

I had always been a sucker for buffets, and I attributed my passion for "all you can eat" menus to being in an orphanage.

Given my love of food, it's a surprise that I don't weigh more. Now--- on the eve of my cancer diagnosis and in preparation for the invasive surgery to remove almost a foot of my colon---I am being told 'no food or drink for two days'.

I wished I had stored away some raisins.

chapter 2

MAHALO

I was raised in the state of Ohio and there were not many Asians living in the area where I grew up. The kids at school were completely oblivious to where I came from, and they assumed that I was either Chinese or Japanese. They had never heard of Korea and I was the only Korean student in the school. It was a challenge growing up and looking different from the other children.

Ethnic slurs and name-calling of Jap, chink, and pancake face were chanted to me. The wide-eyed children would take their fingers to their faces and make them slant-eyed as they walked past me.

Fortunately, my parents instilled an extraordinary love in me from the first time they held me in their arms. When I would come home crying after being teased at school, my mother would cradle and hug me. She would wipe away the tears from my face and tell me, "We chose you and no matter what anyone says, you are special and loved."

The name-calling wore off as time passed and the bullies became bored and left me alone. The fact that I had three older brothers protecting me might have also been a factor to them finding other targets.

Being the only girl in the family, my mother wanted to dress me up in pink ribbons and to play with dolls. To her disappointment, I preferred to play cops and robbers with the boys in my grass stained jeans instead. I was the quintessential tomboy.

When I was finished with school, I headed west in search of an adventure. I drove my car from Ohio up to Alaska. I got a job on an Alaskan salmon fishing boat for the summer to make some money.

Working as a deckhand on the fishing boat, was hard and the days were long. My hands were swollen from gutting fish all day and my feet were always cold and wet from the frigid seawater that splashed onto the boat deck. Weeks out at sea with no showers, the blood and fish scales would be caked in my oily knotted hair. They were miserable days filled with agonizing labor and restless nights, but I loved it.

After the fishing season was over, I ended up driving off the road and crashed my car. It was totaled. There went my plans of driving back to Ohio. But I was young and free, nothing could stop me. I was ready for whatever came next, up for any new adventure.

I remembered people on the boat had talked about working in Alaska for the summer and going to Hawaii for the winter. They would fly down to the islands and get jobs waiting tables at the resorts. In my mind, avoiding the cold winter and learning how to surf seemed like the most logical thing to do.

I called home and my mother answered. "Mom, I'm not coming back to Ohio. I just bought a one-way ticket to Hawaii and a bathing suit!"

"Really, Sarah? You don't know a single soul out there, Why do you need to be so far away? What if something happens to you?"

"It's going to be fine, I'm a big girl. I can take care of myself."

She knew how stubborn I was and that there was no point in arguing with me. "Do you remember when you used to tell people that you were from Hawaii?" she asked.

When I was little. I made up a story that I was Hawaiian so the kids would not tease me. "Yes, mom, I remember."

She was worried but I could hear a small tinge of excitement in her voice, "You promise to call when you land?"

"Of course, I love you." I said, as I hung up the phone.

I was twenty-two years old when I landed in Honolulu on the island of Oahu. It's the state capital and a bustling big city. I was overwhelmed by all of the people and wanted a slower pace. The locals advised me to try another island, Maui maybe.

The next day, I took a short twenty-minute flight over to Maui. The locals say, "Maui No Ka OI" which translates Maui is the best and it rang true for me. I fell in love with the island's welcoming warmth and abundance of beauty. I felt the "Aloha spirit." The island was filled with colorful flowers, waterfalls, and pristine beaches. The post cards don't lie, it is paradise.

Upon my arrival, I discovered that Hawaii was diverse with culture and people. It was known as the melting pot of the Pacific. Along with the first Polynesians settlers, there was also a rich history of immigration throughout the islands. I noticed a large Asian population and influence in the state. Like the story of the ugly duckling, I had found my place.

My guidebook led me to a backpacker youth hostel. I checked in without much thought, not imagining that it would be my home for the next five years. The first week I stayed there, I was given a job.

The hostel ran a work exchange program. You would work a few hours a day in housekeeping, reception, landscaping, or tour guiding and in return, you were given free accommodations.

At the hostel, I met backpackers and travelers from all over the world. My days were filled with surfing at the beach or hiking in the rain forest. At night, there were parties where I danced and drank the time away. It was there where I met the most important person in my life: my husband, Roland.

We had a saying at the hostel: "You never know who is going to check in, in the next hour."

On a sunny September day, a young man from Switzerland checked in. I saw Roland the first morning he was there, and it wasn't love at first sight. It was lust at first sight. He was tall, blond, and handsome. I looked on the guest register and saw that he was only staying for a week. I had to act fast, so I flirted for a few days, which turned out to be quite difficult since the recipient of my attentions did not speak fluent English and I did not speak a word of German.

After the third night of flirting, I was frustrated and decided to make a move. Roland and some guests of the hostel were outside sitting on a picnic table laughing and drinking. It was getting late and they started to head inside to go to their rooms. As Roland walked past me, I cornered him and pushed him up against the wall. I leaned into him and asked, "Do you know what this means?"

There was a confused look on his face, and he said, "No."

I kissed him. "Do you know what this means now?"

He smiled and said, "Yes."

Roland had planned to visit the other Hawaiian Islands after Maui, but decided to extend his stay at the hostel after that night. He had three weeks' vacation and as the days passed, filled with scenic hikes, long swims, and hanging out with the other hostel guests, our fun holiday fling was turning into much more. We were inseparable young lovers and the language barrier did not stop us from connecting. Although, there were times when it did create some confusing conversations.

Lying in bed one evening, Roland stared at my legs and said, "You have ugly legs."

My mouth was wide open, "Excuse me? What did you say?"

"Your legs, look they are ugly."

I started to slap him in the arm, and he pointed to the dirt on the side of my calf. I laughed. "You mean dirty?"

His face lit up, "Yes, dirty!"

The weeks passed and our time together was rapidly coming to an end. I had fallen for him hard, my first real love. Everything felt right, but in a few days, Roland would be on the other side of the world.

The night before he left for Switzerland, we went skinny-dipping at a secluded beach. The sky was pitch black and the ocean was warm. We held each other in the water, and I said, "I love this place."

He kissed me and said, "I love you, too."

I knew he made mistakes with words, but this was not a mistake. My heart was racing, and the words flew out of my mouth, "I love you, too!"

chapter 3

MAN & WIFE

Over the next year, we had a whirlwind, long-distance romance. It became apparent that we could not be apart from each other much longer. Roland quit his job in Switzerland and flew to Maui for good. He moved halfway around the world for me, and when he arrived at the airport, we jumped into each other's arms.

The time flew by, and Roland's tourist visa that allowed him to stay in the United States for six months was expiring soon. We had talked about getting married, and I contacted an immigration lawyer to find out what steps we needed to take for Roland to stay in America. Over the phone, the lawyer said, "You have to get married as soon as possible. Here is a list of names and numbers, call me when you're hitched."

I started dialing all the numbers and arranged to pick up the marriage license the same day. We made an appointment to get married at the courthouse the next morning.

That evening, Roland came out of the bathroom with a towel wrapped around his waist. He grabbed my arm and got down on his knee and said, "Will you marry me and be my wife?"

"Yes! Wait! Holy crap, you have to ask my dad for his permission."

In that moment, I realized I had forgotten to call my parents to let them know that I was getting married. I grabbed the phone and took a deep breath. My mother answered the phone and I said, "Mom, I know this is going to surprise you, but I'm getting married tomorrow at the courthouse."

"Excuse me, what?"

I knew I had some explaining to do but did not want to get into the details. "Roland and I are getting married. Can I talk to dad?"

"You never mentioned marriage, wedding..."

I cut her off, "Can you get dad?"

My father's voice came over the phone. "Sarah, now what in the world is going on? Your mother said you are getting married?"

"Yes, dad. I'm going to give the phone to Roland, so you can give him your permission."

I thrust the phone in Roland's direction. He had never met or spoken to my parents before and did not want to talk to my father, but knew he had no choice. He sheepishly said, "Hello."

My dad began to cry, "Well, I hear you are going to marry my daughter and yes, you have my blessing and I love you."

My parents were elated for the two of us and we went to bed excited for the big day ahead of us.

It was a hot humid morning when we arrived at the courthouse. A judge was to officiate our wedding. She was our very own version of a no-nonsense type of Japanese Judge Judy: small in stature, but her black gown and wire-framed glasses gave her a commanding presence.

We stood in front of her, as she began the wedding ceremony. The judge turned to Roland and said, "Repeat after me. I Roland, take you Sarah to be my wife, to have and to hold from this day forward, for better, for worse, for richer, for poorer, in sickness and in health, to love and cherish till death do us part."

Roland's face turned white with fear, his English was not that good. He looked at the judge and nervously asked, "Can you please say that again?"

I couldn't control myself and burst into laughter. Immediately, the judge frowned, "This is a serious matter. Do you know what you are repeating?"

Roland clearly intimidated by the judge sweetly answered back, "Yes, but can you say it a little slower for me?"

It took some patience on the judge's part, but we made it through our vows. Finishing up the ceremony she said, "Now the exchange of the rings will be made."

My face cringed, "Oh, we don't have any rings," I said.

We were going to have tattoos made. I could clearly see from her facial expression that she did not approve of it, but she continued on. In the end, she sternly looked at Roland and said, "Well, you at least better take her out to a nice restaurant tonight."

A Hawaiian friend of mine created the design for our tattoos on our ring fingers. It featured Hawaiian sea turtles; I had the symbol of a male turtle on my finger, to represent Roland. And on his finger, he had the symbol of a female turtle, representing me. The Hawaiian sea turtles also symbolized our love of the land and sea. They could never be lost or taken off.

We left the hostel and started our new life together. Roland went through the immigration process and he got a job in construction. His English improved and five years later, he became a U.S. citizen. He loved all the opportunities America had to offer, and after years of working construction for someone else, he decided to start his own company. We became proud business owners, and Roland became a licensed contractor in the state of Hawaii.

I held different jobs through the years. I waited tables at a restaurant for a short time and then got a job as a tour guide, taking the tourists to all of the beautiful spots on the island. Then a job at the airport opened up and I started working for an airline company. I was assigned to work on the ramp and helped load the planes with the luggage and cargo.

After years of hard work, we were able to afford a house and get a dog. Our house was in a nice subdivision on the island's north shore, a cute three-bedroom, two-bath house on a quaint cul-da-sac.

It was walking distance to the little beach town of Paia, which was known as a hippy surfer town filled with unique boutiques and restaurants. We could ride our bikes to the beach and take afternoon strolls on the sand.

When we first moved in, we planted fruit trees everywhere. We had lemons, limes, tangerines, bananas, papaya, star fruit, passion fruit, and coconuts in our yard. Roland built an outdoor shower that watered the banana trees and there was a white picket fence in the front yard. We were living the American dream.

On nights when the moon was full, Roland and I would often go to the beach and lie down on the sand. The reflection of the moon on the water lit up the night sky. We would lie close together and discuss our hopes and dreams for the future. While we watched the silhouettes of the palm trees swaying in the wind, I would stare at the moon, thinking about how lucky we were to live in Hawaii.

chapter 4

A WALK IN THE PARK

Roland and I did not have kids. We had a dog named, Doodle. People thought that Doodle was an Australian Shepard because of his size, floppy ears, and brown and white fur, but our pride and joy was just a lovable mutt.

Doodle loved car rides, and every morning I drove him to the beach. I would let him stick his head out of the car window and I cheerfully would watch his tail wag back and forth. When we drove past the surfers in the parking lot, they would give Doodle the "hang loose" sign with their hands and smile.

I spoiled Doodle with car rides and long afternoon walks. There was a large park in our neighborhood, where people would take their dogs for walks. The park was spacious and had soccer and baseball fields for the kids to play. It also had a view of the surrounding green sugar cane fields and the beautiful slopes of the volcano, Haleakala.

One late afternoon in October, I walked to the park with Doodle. It was dusk and the sun had slipped behind the West Maui Mountains. A black Labrador retriever ran up to us, and his owner approached me with a smile. She was tall and athletic looking with her long brown hair pulled back. There was an effortless beauty to her, and I was a little awestruck at first. "Hi, this is Kai," she said with a smile.

I smiled back and said, "Hi, this is Doodle. He is friendly."

I thought it was funny, how dog owners introduced their dogs before themselves. Doodle and Kai started sniffing around and marking their territory.

The woman was wearing a blue tank top, and I noticed a medical patch on her skin near her shoulder. "Hi, I'm Emalia," she said.

"I'm Sarah."

She caught me looking at her medical patch, and she put her hand over it. "Oh, this is for my treatment."

"Oh, I'm sorry for staring."

She smiled and nodded. "No, it's okay. I have cancer. This is for my chemotherapy."

"Oh, wow, I'm so sorry to hear that. What kind of cancer do you have, if you don't mind me asking?"

"Colon cancer."

"Are you ok?" I knew it was a rude to ask and I was embarrassed but also stunned as she was so young. I had always thought colon cancer affected older people. I hoped I hadn't offended her.

She let out a laugh, which was a relief, and seemed very open to talk about her cancer. There was a special warmth about her, the kind that made you feel instantly at ease.

She went on to explain, "I had this bruising on my stomach. I went to the doctor and had some tests done. The next thing I know I'm being told that I have stage-four colon cancer. I asked the doctor how many stages there are? He said there are only four."

I was in disbelief, and she continued, "So now I'm doing chemotherapy and I'm going to beat this thing."

I somehow managed to reply, "I'm shocked. I'm sorry. I mean look at you. You're young and fit. How does this happen?"

She laughed, "I know, really." She paused for a moment and turned to me and said, "What surprises life gives you."

Then, she pointed out to her young son playing in the grass. She was a mother. My heart dropped and I was stunned all over again. Doodle started barking, and I had to go calm him. As I walked away, I said, "I'm so sorry. It was nice to meet you. Good luck with everything."

It was dark and the streetlights were turning on when I arrived home. My conversation with Emalia left me feeling deeply sad and unsettled. I couldn't stop thinking about the pain she must be enduring and how devastating it must be to receive a diagnosis that turns your whole world upside down.

I filled Doodle's bowl with kibble and started to cook dinner. Roland came home from work and gave me a kiss on the cheek and said, "Hi, honey, how was your day?"

I barely responded, and he could sense something was up. "What's wrong?" He asked.

An overwhelming feeling of sadness came over me and my voice trembled, "I just met this beautiful young mother at the park who is fighting for her life and she might die."

"What?"

"Yeah, she has stage-four colon cancer. It's heartbreaking."

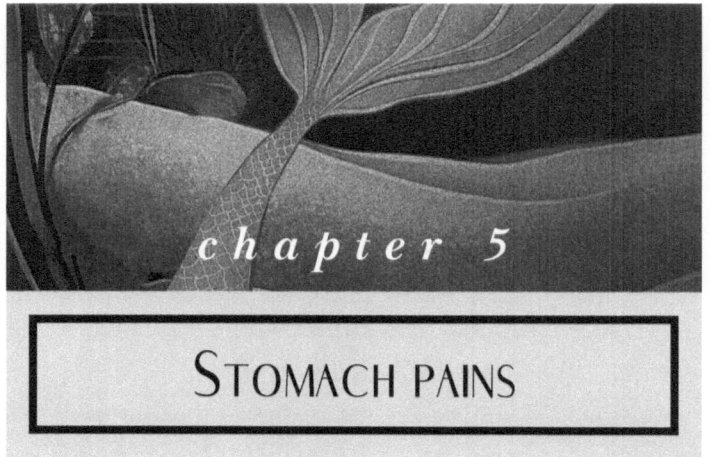

chapter 5

STOMACH PAINS

I worked at the major airport on the island, located in the city of Kahului. It was a bustling place, full of energy. Tourists and locals, all carrying boarding passes and suitcases, passed by me as I made my way into work, each heading off to their next destination.

I was at the time clock and my friend Julie had arrived. She was out of breath from running and racing to punch in. "Out of my way! I don't want to be late!"

She barely made it in time and was laughing hysterically, explaining why she was running late. Our friend, Grace walked up to the both of us and sarcastically said, "It's going to be a fun day of work! There are already two delayed planes and a mechanical issue."

Hearing the news, my stomach burned, "I think this place is giving me an ulcer," I said as I rubbed a pain in my stomach.

Grace laughed, "Yeah, I wouldn't be surprised."

Julie hit me in the arm, "Sarah, I'm always telling you to stop being so stressed out all of the time."

"I worry too much, I know."

Smiling back at the two of them, I said, "Well, if it is an ulcer, I might get a few weeks off of work."

—~——

I hated going to the doctor and always tried to avoid it, but Roland insisted I make an appointment and get it checked out. After I finally went, the doctor told me I had colitis; an inflammation of the colon and there would be no time off of work and I was prescribed some medication.

Weeks past and the pain in my stomach went away. The medicine worked and I thought to myself, "Problem solved."

It was short lived, and the pain returned. I was on the night shift and arrived at the airport feeling lousy and nauseous. I had not had a bowel movement for two days and I was quite bloated. After an hour, the bulge in my stomach was extremely painful and my supervisor allowed me to leave work early.

Once home, I took my work clothes off and hopped in the shower. The hot water massaging my back and head felt wonderful. Roland was worried about me, but I assured him that I was fine. I went to bed, thinking that the pain would be gone in the morning.

It ended up being a horrible night. My stomach felt and looked like a big bloated balloon. I tossed and turned, trying to get comfortable, but my whole body was aching.

In the morning, I felt weak and everything hurt. Concerned, Roland pleaded with me, "Sarah, I've never seen you in pain like this. Please go to the doctor today."

"No, I'm fine, I'm sure I'll go to the bathroom soon, and everything will be okay."

All morning, I sat on the toilet and nothing happened. I felt nauseous and started to throw up. The phone rang; it was Roland calling from work. "Sarah, did you go to the bathroom yet? Are you feeling any better?"

"I'm still sick, I've been throwing up all morning. I can't hold anything down. Roland, I don't know what is wrong with me."

I could hear the panic in his voice, "I'm coming home right now and I'm taking you to the emergency room."

The ER doctor wore glasses and had a slightly cold bedside manner. He snapped on a blue latex glove and stuck his finger in my rear end before plainly stating, "You're distended and constipated."

He prescribed GoLYTELY, the fluid that you take prior to a colonoscopy and said, "This should clear you out."

Roland and I picked up the prescription at the pharmacy and went home. The medicine was disgusting; I was barely able to swallow it. My body was shaking, and I started to throw up again. I was exhausted and dehydrated. So, we got in the car and drove back to the emergency room.

I was lying in an ER bed and Roland was pacing back and forth in the room. He was making me nervous and I asked him to sit down. He sat in the chair next to the bed and looked at me, "Sarah, what is going on? Why are you so sick? My mind has been racing all day. What if you have cancer?"

My heart sank, I felt terrible for putting him through all of this. He had lost both of his parents at a young age and now thought he might lose his wife. "Honey, I don't have cancer. You always think the worst. I'm going to be fine. We are going to live a long life together. Really."

A female doctor pulled the hospital curtain to the side and appeared next to the bed. I was relieved that it was not the same doctor from the morning. I had some blood tests done and she ordered a CAT scan for me. A nurse came into the room and instructed me to change into a hospital gown. I put my clothes and personal belongings in a plastic bag and had my CAT scan.

When the results were ready, the doctor sat down next to me. Looking me in the eyes, she said, "Well, from what it looks like, you either have colitis or colon cancer."

Of course, I thought and answered, "Yes, I was told I had colitis and was prescribed some medicine and it went away."

She looked down at her chart and with restraint in her voice said, "Colitis and colon cancer look very similar on a CAT scan."

I was listening to the doctor but all I could think of was *cancer.* Roland was holding my hand and he began to cry. Colon cancer. *How is this possible?* I thought of the woman from the park, Emalia. *How can this be happening?*

She continued, "We are going to send you up to a hospital room and have you meet with the surgeon in the morning."

She got up and left the room. *What hospital room?* I thought, *This is a joke, right? This is not really happening to me. I'm supposed to be fine and go back home.* I looked at Roland and tears were streaming down his face. My face was numb, and an overwhelming fear came over me.

chapter 6

YOU ARE SO LUCKY

A nurse entered the room and she asked Roland to leave. I let go of his hand and listened as she gave him directions on how to get to my hospital room. It was located in another wing of the building and he had to take the elevator. On his way out, Roland said, "I'll be waiting for you in your room. I love you."

I put my hand up and gave him a halfhearted wave goodbye and watched him leave. Lying on the bed, I watched the nurse go over to a cabinet against the wall. She grabbed some items out of the cabinet and placed them on a tray next to my bed. She sat me up and said, "Please, open your mouth as wide as you can."

It wasn't the dentist's office and I was clueless as to why I needed to open my mouth, but I obeyed and opened my mouth. She took a bottle that looked like a spray can and squirted a chemical into my mouth. The fluid went all the way up into my nose and sinuses.

"It's a numbing agent," she said.

I didn't say anything and politely nodded back at her. She took a long clear plastic tube that was sitting on the tray and held it in her hand. "Open up again please," she said.

I opened my mouth and she shoved the plastic tube down my nose all the way to my stomach. I had no idea what was going on and she said, "This is called an NG tube. It's going to suck up the stuff that won't come out the other end."

My throat was scratched from the plastic tube and I could barely talk. I swallowed hard and managed to speak. "Thank you," I said.

An orderly walked into the room and it was time for me to go to my hospital room. She transported me through the hospital corridors, and we took the elevator up to my room. Roland was sitting in a chair, in the corner of the room, waiting for my arrival.

I was transferred from the gurney onto the bed. A nurse hooked up my NG tube to a machine. The machine made a sucking noise and brown liquid started moving through the plastic tube into a canister next to my bed.

Roland stood up and held my hand, while I checked out my new surroundings. I had a private room in the new wing of the hospital. There was a large glass window with an ocean view and a television. My bed had a control panel where I could push a button for the nurses to come and another button to move my bed up and down. I could see the worry in Roland's eyes, and tried to comfort him. I said, "This is better than a hotel!"

It had been a long day and I was tired and really hungry. Sadly, I was informed that there was to be no food or liquids allowed until further notice. I felt the tube down my throat and the IV in my arm, but it was like a dream, none of it felt real. A nurse came into the room and gave me some painkillers and I dozed off with Roland by my side.

After numerous tests and two days of no eating or drinking the surgeon informed me, it was indeed colon cancer. The tumor created a blockage in my colon and that was what caused me to get so sick.

Roland was devastated when he heard the news and excused himself. The idea of my life being over started to creep into my consciousness, and I pushed it away. But it didn't stop the tears from falling. I lay in my hospital bed crying and confused.

Roland broke the news to my parents and brothers. Naturally, my mother and father wanted to fly out to see me. I assured them that I would be fine, and I did not want them to come. It would have been too much for me to handle at the time and they respected my wishes.

My two best friends from work, Grace and Julie visited. Julie watched Doodle while I was in the hospital and at my direction, Grace informed my employer of my condition. They were both in complete and utter shock of my diagnosis. I tried to lighten the mood and joked, "Well, it wasn't an ulcer after all. Looks like I won't be at work for a while."

I was soon getting prepped and ready for my four-hour surgery to remove the tumor. Roland held my hand as the nurses buzzed around hooking different machines to me and giving me injections of drugs. As they started to roll the gurney out of the room he followed and never let go of my hand. I watched him look at me and thought about the wonderful life we had together.

Heading into the elevator, was where Roland and I parted ways. We exchanged our "I love you's," and I gave him a weak smile and said, "See you in a few hours."

All he could do was nod and he kissed me on my forehead. The elevator doors shut, and I thought about Emalia. When I would ask myself, *"Why me? Of all the people to get cancer, why me?"* I thought of her. I stopped feeling sorry for myself and knew I was not alone. I saw that she was positive and brave. And, in that moment, she inspired me. I told myself, *I'm not done, I can be strong too.*

The operating room was like a NASCAR pit station, and everyone there had a purpose. Lying next to me was a large tray filled with surgical instruments and tools. I stared at the examination light above my head and a nurse approached me. She started to recite a backwards countdown and before she got to seven, I was out like a light.

Five hours later, I woke up in a fog. I opened my eyes, and Roland jumped up from the chair in my room. He kissed me with tears in his eyes, and I smiled. We were silent and as I looked into his weary eyes, I knew everything was going to be ok.

Roland left to get coffee and a young nurse came in to check on me. She was a travelling nurse from Kentucky and had big blue eyes and red curly hair. She couldn't contain herself and quickly blurted out, "You are so lucky!"

"Excuse me? I'm sorry what did you say?" I was confused.

"I watched your husband before you went in for surgery. He looked at you with so much love. I only wish I could find someone that loved me that much."

I smiled and thought about how amazing my husband was. Roland was not only the most caring man I had ever met, but also very handsome. Friends told him that he looked like a hunky movie star and women often asked me how I got such a babe. How did I, the girl who never got asked to prom or have a boyfriend in high school, get so lucky?

When she left the room, I felt a pain in my bladder. To my dismay, I had a catheter, a plastic tube inserted in my urethra so my urine could be collected in a bag. The surgeon agreed to remove it but informed me that unless I urinated within the next twelve hours, she would have to put it back in.

For the rest of the day I had the feeling of wanting to pee, and yet nothing happened. Time ticked away, and the day passed. I didn't want them to stick the catheter back in me, but it was starting to look like I wouldn't have a choice.

After my last attempt to pee, I got up from the toilet and turned on the faucet to wash my hands. As the warm water hit my skin, I felt the sensation that I was about to pee. I yelled for Roland to grab the small bucket on the floor and hold it under me. We were quite a sight: Roland kneeling beneath me with a plastic bucket, while I stood by the sink with warm water running over my hands. It worked like a dream and came out like a waterfall.

So, there we stood, the same two people that had fallen in love at a youth hostel in paradise, now just as in love but in a hospital bathroom. Roland looked up at me and said, "For better, for worse, in sickness and in health," and we both laughed.

chapter 7

HEY KIDDO

The surgeon came into the room and sat down beside my bed. She gave us details about how the surgery went. We were informed that I had Stage 3 colon cancer, and nine inches of my colon and the tumor had been removed. The tumor had broken the colon wall, and three of twenty-three lymph nodes contained cancerous cells. I would need at least six months of chemotherapy.

I tried to hold back my tears and be strong, but I was shaking as I thanked her. The thought that even after the surgery, this wasn't over, that my future was still uncertain was overwhelming. I did my best to compose myself and put on a brave face for everyone.

The surgeon informed me that I had to stay in the hospital for another week to recover from the surgery.

Fortunately for me, they were able to do a laparoscopic surgery, which was, less invasive and left only small scars.

The surgeon left and Roland was in disbelief and said, "Six months of chemotherapy? Is this nightmare going to end?"

"Honey, we will deal with it day by day."

"Do you know what chemotherapy is? They are going to poison you! You're going to be sick for six months!"

"Roland, I don't have a choice, I have to do it. Let's not talk about it right now. I'm exhausted."

He kissed me on the forehead, and I told him to get some sleep and I would see him in the morning.

The next day, my friend Dylan came by the hospital for a visit. From previous conversations we'd had, I knew that he worked with Emalia's husband. I asked him to help me get in touch with her and explained to him that I wanted to thank Emalia. Although I had only met her briefly, she changed my perspective on colon cancer.

I was only thirty-seven, and everyone had been telling me how young I was for a colon cancer diagnosis. But I knew that Emalia was also young and that there was no genuine target age. Having heard her story gave me courage and helped me understand the disease invading my body. It gave me strength knowing that I wasn't alone in this battle.

He was quiet and said he would pass my message along.

That same day our dear friend Cindy came to visit. I could hear her before I saw her as, she was chattering away out in the hallway. She walked in the room, hugged me and said, "Hey kiddo, you sure scared all of us!"

Roland had met Cindy years earlier while doing construction work on her house. She and her husband, Jim, had retired and moved from the mainland to Maui, where they bought a home and hired Roland to remodel it. Cindy adored his charming accent, and they hit it off immediately.

I thought it was endearing, that my husband's close friend was an older retired woman. Cindy was in her late fifties and was born with the gift of gab. She could talk for hours and there was a fun, energetic quality about her. She was well dressed and in excellent shape for her age; you could tell she took pride in her appearance.

Hanging out with Cindy was like stepping back in time or being in an episode of *Mad Men*. She and Jim were the martini-drinking type; a type that didn't exist in the world I came from. She grew up in the Midwest, and when she was old enough, she packed her car and drove west. She described herself as a "gal Friday" in the marketing world back in the early eighties.

Her dialogue was from a time and place I had never known. She used expressions like, "Three sheets to the wind," or "Here's mud in your eye." Everyone was "kiddo." It struck me as reminiscent of *the Great Gatsby's* "old sport." She greeted everyone with a chipper, "Hey kiddo!" Cindy had the charm and charisma to make anyone she met feel special. She was the kind of person that lit up a room when she entered it.

She and Jim lived close to the hospital and Roland had slept at their house for a few nights to be closer to me in case anything happened. Cindy started laughing and launched into a story about how she had to fill their fridge with "deer piss," her term for Roland's cheap beer.

Then she casually mentioned how she had experienced a pain in her stomach while doing her sit-ups that morning. "Maybe I have a hernia," she laughed, "from all those sit ups."

"You should get that checked out," I said, remembering how I had thought my own pain was an ulcer.

"Don't be silly, it's nothing."

"Well, you know..." She interrupted me and tried to make a joke, "What, maybe I have what you have?"

"Cindy, that's not funny."

Trying to change the subject, I began to tell her about my new plans for the next six months: chemotherapy. She said, "Well, I'm taking you to your chemo treatments. I'm going to pick you up and drop you off for all of them."

I said, "Cindy, that is not necessary. They say a lot of people drive themselves."

"That's a bunch of hogwash. You can't drive yourself. It's already settled. I'm taking you to your treatments."

I clearly didn't have much say in the matter and knew there was no point in arguing with Cindy. She made up her mind and that was that.

chapter 8

FINDING DORA

I was getting tired of being in the hospital. Every few hours, a nurse came by to take blood samples and the janitors came twice a day to empty the garbage bins and to clean the bathroom. There was a constant stream of visitors, nurses, cleaners, and general noise. It was non-stop commotion.

On the bright side, I had access to a button that released morphine into my body through my IV. I was in a lot of pain from the surgery and the drugs made all of my pain go away. After my surgery, I no longer had the NG tube in my stomach, and I was finally able to eat and drink again.

My stomach and colon were delicate, so I had to start by eating bland foods like Jello and plain toast. A few days later, I was allowed "real" hospital food. The meals from the hospital were okay. The food looked and tasted like it came from a school cafeteria. I wasn't going to complain after not eating for such a long time, but I planned to have a big juicy steak when I was discharged.

Roland came in the room with a smile and a green concoction in his hand and proudly said, "I brought you a green spinach smoothie."

I was disappointed, not just a little but super disappointed. I had been dreaming of something delicious to eat since I had been in the hospital. I wanted him to bring me something good, like a cheeseburger and some french fries. Annoyed, I said, "That's what you brought me to eat?"

"Yes, it's going to be our new thing. Healthy living! I had a long conversation with Dora last night."

Roland handed me the green smoothie and I took a tentative sip. "Who is Dora?"

"She was a client I had a few years ago. I remembered a conversation I had with her and so I called her last night."

Dora lived in Portland. She was in her fifties and was a small spitfire of a woman. She had a condo on Maui that she stayed in twice a year. When Roland remodeled her shower, he passed by the kitchen and saw herbs, powders, supplements, and vegetables all over the counter. They began talking about food and he listened to her amazing story.

Almost a decade earlier, Dora was diagnosed with stage four cervical cancer. The doctors would not treat her with chemo or radiation. They said she was too far-gone, and that she should go and live out her last months of life.

That wasn't what Dora wanted to hear. She planned to live a long, full life, and so she changed her entire diet, and studied everything she could about cancer. It was a miracle that she was able to cure herself. She would offer help to anyone who would listen to how she did it, and Roland was determined that I listen.

"Do I really have to drink this?" I asked.

"Honey, drink it for me. It's going to help you when you go through chemo, and I'm going to start drinking smoothies with you too."

Roland had a new goal in life: to help me beat cancer through food. I did not want to crush his enthusiasm, so I reluctantly smiled and drank the smoothie. Sadly, my plan of devouring a steak disappeared in that moment.

———

When I arrived home from the hospital, Doodle jumped up and licked my face, tail wagging with excitement. Friends stopped by with flowers and balloons, filling the house with warmth and care. I was still on painkillers and in the midst of healing, but it was a comforting homecoming. Most of all, I was grateful to finally sleep in my own bed.

I had been anxious to see Dylan in particular to ask about Emalia. I wanted to know how she was doing, to share my story and uncanny diagnosis, and to thank her for inspiring me during our brief conversation. When Dylan got off work he came by for a visit, I was eager to see if he got her phone number for me.

"Did you talk to Emalia's husband?" I asked.

Dylan looked at me, but wouldn't look me in the eyes. His head lowered and he looked down at the floor.

"I didn't want to tell you while you were in the hospital, but Emalia died. I'm sorry."

I was in shock and the tears started to well up. I stood there and started crying for a woman I barely knew. I cried for the pain she must have gone through. I cried for her family. I cried because I didn't know why all of this was happening.

chapter 9

WE ARE WHAT WE EAT

In the children's book *Charlotte's Web*, I loved the rat named Templeton. He ate everything, and his night of gluttony at the fair was my favorite part of the story. The idea of eating funnel cakes and deep-fried sweets made me happy.

I grew up on a typical Midwestern American diet. I loved the sugary cereals with colored marshmallows for breakfast. For lunch, I had the boxed juices, bologna sandwiches with American cheese and mayonnaise on white bread. Sloppy Joe's and spaghetti were standard meals for dinner, and I was addicted to soda.

At the hostel, I drank beer, ate ramen noodles, pizza and hot dogs. When Roland and I got married, I began cooking similar meals that I had grown up with. I made beef stroganoff, tuna fish casserole and steak and potatoes. We did not eat a lot of fast food and I was not overweight. I never dieted or worried about what foods I put into my body. In my mind, I ate healthy. Dora was quick to inform me otherwise.

Roland studied everything, asked questions, and believed that changing our diet was what I needed to beat cancer permanently. I knew he felt lost and powerless, and that this was his way of helping me. He took charge of the kitchen, and we changed what we ate. He emailed and called Dora constantly to get her advice on everything. Roland had a new mantra of, "Dora does this, Dora does that..."

She was happy to help and under her guidance, we kept our sugar intake to a minimum and limited it to only natural sources, like fruit and honey. At the supermarket, we had to check all of the food labels because Dora warned us that if something contained more than five ingredients it was no good.

Roland started making green smoothies full of sprouts, kale, spinach, collard greens, apples, lemons and bananas for us every morning. We took Dora's advice and bought a Vitamix blender; a cheap thirty-dollar blender would not do. The shiny new machine was the most expensive thing in our kitchen.

In the mornings, I would wake up to the sound of the blender and there were times when I hated it. It wasn't the sound of the motor that bothered me, but the noise was a reminder that I had cancer. My body failed me and now I was forced to live with this diet the rest of my life. I didn't like all of the food restrictions and at times I was like a child, hands clenched thinking, *Nobody else has to eat this way, so why do I have to.*

Roland was strict with our new healthy lifestyle, and I did not have much of a say when it came to what we ate. If I suggested eating something "bad," like a dessert, he would get upset and lecture me on how bad sugar was for me. I knew he was doing it out of love, but at times, it irritated me, how easy the diet was for him. He had always been more disciplined then me. He started his mornings by running and doing push-ups and squats, whereas, I would cuddle with Doodle and drink my morning coffee on the couch.

I knew in my heart that eating healthy was important, not only for my relationship but for myself. The thought of dying scared me. There was so much more I wanted to do in life, and I was supposed to grow old with my husband.

There were a few exceptions to my diet. Dora told Roland that I was not supposed to drink alcohol or eat chocolate unless I was really on edge. That usually occurred on days close to my period.

"I have Dora's permission," I said with a grin on my face and a glass of wine in my hand the first time it happened. Roland was annoyed but he knew better then, to say anything.

It became easier to eat healthy as the time passed and we got into a routine. We had a green smoothie for both breakfast and lunch every day, and a "real" dinner of fish and rice, or some form of a vegan meal. No more red meat, bacon, chicken, or turkey. Processed food was out; sugary sweets, gone. We did allow ourselves to have pizza once a week. It was our one indulgence, because a life without pizza seemed too horrible.

We also lived in one of the best places in the world to change our diet. Hawaii was a nutritionist's heaven, with its tropical weather and rich volcanic soil, the fruits and vegetables were bountiful. We had a local health food store in our town with reasonable prices, and there were year-round local farmer's markets with fresh vegetables and fruit. Our friends dropped off bananas, avocados, and mangos from their yards at our door. Most of the restaurants in our town had healthy options, and there was a new raw food restaurant that had recently opened up.

Dora was an amazing woman with the spirit to live, and the diet was not easy for her, either. She avoided hotels that offered breakfast buffets, as the temptation was too great. When I struggled with my desire for a cheeseburger, she would tell me, "When I go hiking and get to the top of the mountain, I can breathe in and say, "I'm alive. Skipping the doughnuts and processed foods is worth it."

chapter 10

BUDDY

The start date for my chemotherapy was getting closer and I had an appointment with my surgeon to get my "port" put in at the hospital. A port, I learned, is a small plastic knob they install in patient's chests, connected to a vein, to deliver medicine, nutrients, or, in my case, chemo. It is easier than having to stick an IV in your arm every time you go in for treatment.

It was a quick procedure and the port felt funny. I rubbed my hand along it to feel this foreign object in my body. It was placed below my collarbone and stuck out like a nipple. In the mirror, I began to stare at myself. I remembered the medical patch on Emalia, that was over her port in the same area.

The next day, I walked out to the mailbox, and a small furry black dog came running down the street. He didn't have a leash on, and his owner was nowhere in sight. I tried to call him over. I hoped he would get close enough to me so I could grab him. He came inches away from me but as soon as I made a move, he ran away.

Doodle was inside the house, barking up a storm. I went in the house and got a dog treat out of the kitchen cabinet. I was going to lure the little pooch into our fenced-in yard with food. It worked, and I was able to corner him and look at his dog tag. He was from a house up the street, so I picked him up and carried him back to his home.

His owner was outside doing yard work. I approached the woman and said, "Your dog was down our street, and I brought him back for you."

It was a hot day, and her grey hair was pulled back in a ponytail. She looked up from the lawn and said, "Oh, that's just Buddy. We got him a few months ago. I wasn't looking to get a dog, but somehow, I wound up at the Humane Society. And when you fall in love, you don't have a choice, and I fell in love with Buddy. He runs around the neighborhood, but always finds his way back home." She chuckled and patted some dirt off her shorts and said, "I'm Anne by the way."

"Hi, I'm Sarah," I said.

I looked up at the house and it had been newly painted. The house had been under major renovations for the last few months, and Roland and I had been watching the progress with interest. I said, "I like the color you picked for the house."

"Thanks. It's finally almost finished," she said.

She and her husband had bought the house years ago, and they had rented it out in the past, because they lived in Maine. Her husband was retiring soon, and they were getting ready to move to Maui fulltime.

They wanted more space for visiting family and friends, so they were converting their three-bedroom, single-story house into a two-story, four-bedroom home.

We continued talking about the home renovations and I told her about my recent hospital stay and my cancer diagnosis. "I got my port put in yesterday," I said.

Anne pulled down her shirt collar and said, "I have a port too."

I stared at her port and I was shocked and surprised. I winced and was afraid to ask but did anyways, "Do you have cancer?"

"I used to a long time ago. When I was in my twenties, I had Hodgkin's lymphoma cancer. Back then; they just radiated the crap out of you. All of my hair fell out in one day. I cried for days after that. I survived but I have had health issues from the radiation ever since. I have this port to help me get proper nutrition."

I was relieved that she didn't have cancer anymore but distraught because of the issues the treatment had caused her. I could tell she was in her fifties and tried to imagine what kind of treatments they gave back in the 1960's and 70's. She was tiny and frail but had a feisty spirited personality. She could see from my face, that I felt sorry for her and changed the subject. "Do you know that when your port is in use, you can't get it wet?" She said.

"Yes, the doctor told me that and suggested I buy some cling wrap, so I could cover my port when I showered."

"Don't use cling wrap. It doesn't stick to the skin very well. Here, come inside the house and I will show you what I use."

I followed her and Buddy into the house and looked around. The interior of the house was remodeled, and the kitchen had new countertops and appliances. Anne opened a drawer and took out a box of what looked like cling wrap, but it read, "Press'n Seal." She held it up and said, "This is what you want to buy."

I thanked her for the advice, and she showed me around the house. She told me to stop by anytime and we exchanged phone numbers. I left the house, thinking about Buddy. I thought, *how funny, if he never came down the street, I might not have ever met Anne.*

chapter 11

6:30

After my cancer diagnosis, 6:30 morning phone calls became a daily ritual between Cindy and me. We were both early risers, up at the crack of dawn. I don't remember the first phone conversation, or who called whom first, but we became much closer.

Before my diagnosis, we would have occasional dinners at Cindy's house and talk once a week. She liked me but loved Roland. Jim and I would sit and listen to them over dinner and their non-stop chattering about politics, construction jobs, and sports. If I mentioned a disagreement between Roland and I, she would always defend him and remind me that he did not grow up with a mother.

Now that we talked every day and all the time, I got to hear all of Cindy's stories and ideas. She never cared about rules and more than once, I wondered if she had been born without a filter. At one point, she insisted that Roland take on a big brother role to her manicurist's son. She pleaded with me to suggest it to him and said, "Her son is only fourteen and a bit on the nerdy side. Roland would be a terrific role model."

"Cindy, that is a crazy idea. First of all, Roland is too busy and slammed with work. And secondly, why would he help your manicurist's son? He doesn't even know them."

In the end, she won, and I brought the idea up to Roland. He laughed and thought it was nuts. Beginning the day, talking with Cindy always put a smile on my face and to me, it was better than a cup of coffee in the morning.

I had a consultation at the cancer clinic with the oncologist and a nurse to go over what I should expect during the chemotherapy and to ask questions. Cindy wanted to pick me up and take me to the appointment. Her volunteering had begun in earnest.

We arrived at the cancer clinic; it was conveniently connected to the hospital and was a fifteen-minute drive from my house. Cindy dropped me off, before parking the car. I checked in at the reception desk and met my oncologist. Afterward, I was led into a back office where I met the nurse who was going to explain my treatment.

I sat alone, at a long conference table and the nurse handed me a checklist of suggested items to get to help with my treatment, ranging from disposable wipes, surgical facemasks, moisturizers and UV protectant clothing.

She took a large book from the shelf. Opening it, she began detailing what I could expect during my treatment. Reading down the list of side effects, everything seemed serious. But then she said, "Expect to have symptoms from your eyes to your anus."

It was the funniest thing I had heard in a long time and I burst out laughing. I was like a little kid hearing a naughty word for the first time. I had uncontrollable giggles and tears in my eyes. The nurse stared at me like I was crazy. I tried to compose myself, but I kept hearing her say, "eyes to anus." Another burst of laughter came out. I desperately tried to compose myself and let the nurse finish explaining everything.

Cindy was waiting for me in the lobby afterwards and reading a magazine. I told her about my debriefing session with the nurse and we got in the car and headed to lunch. We went to a local health food store that had a deli and salad bar.

Cindy opted for a soup and I had a salad. She still had that pain in her abdomen and could feel a lump on her side. "It must be a hernia. I can feel it."

"You know you should go to a doctor."

She squirmed in her chair and said, "I hate doctors."

"Well, so do I, but I'm glad I went to the doctor. By the way, you're sixty years old and need to take care of yourself."

Her mouth fell open. "No, I'm not! I just turned fifty-nine a few months ago."

"Okay, fifty-nine! Did you ever get a colonoscopy?"

Disgust filled her face. "Gross! The idea of them sticking something up there is revolting."

"Cindy, they say you should have one done when you turn fifty. Have one done for me?"

She continued eating and then paused. "Let's talk about something else. But I will think about it," she said.

The next morning, she called me, chipper as always. "Hey kiddo. You'll be happy to know I scheduled a colonoscopy for next month."

"About time!" I said. I was happy that she had actually taken my advice. I was still concerned though. "And what about the hernia?"

"Oh, I'm feeling much better. Don't worry about me. Now on Monday, I will be at your house at 7:30. I think that will give us plenty of time to get to the cancer clinic. You start your chemotherapy at 8:00 right?"

"Yes, I do. I will be waiting for you to pick me up."

With my first chemo session scheduled in just a few days, I was beginning to feel nervous and apprehensive about what to expect. How much hair would I lose? How tired would I be? How sick would I get? All the questions I had were about to get answered.

chapter 12

SERENA THE GOOD WITCH

Cindy pulled into the driveway right on time, 7:30 sharp. I opened the passenger door with a smile. Even though I had resisted the idea at first, I was glad she was driving me to my treatments. It didn't feel so lonely.

Cindy and I arrived at the clinic together and walked in through the double doors. I took a seat and met Serena, my nurse, for the first time. Serena took one look at me, and then looked down on her paper, confused. "Sprecher? Are you German or Swiss?" she said.

"I'm Korean, but my husband is from Switzerland. How did you know?

"I'm Swiss, too," she said with a big smile.

I laughed to myself. What are the odds that I would get a Swiss nurse on the island of Maui?

Serena was a traveling nurse and was relatively new to the island. Her parents had immigrated to the United States from Switzerland when she was a child, and she had grown up in Washington State. She spoke German and knew the town Roland was from.

She was bubbly and in her late twenties. Serena wore bright neon colors, glitter eye shadow, and crystal earrings. She reminded me of a rainbow after a storm. "Some people are drawn together by the universe. It must be fate that we met," she said.

I instantly loved her and could not wait to tell Roland about my Swiss nurse.

Serena and Cindy started talking about Washington and seemed to hit it off right away. Serena's parents lived just outside of Seattle, and coincidentally, Cindy had family there too. In fact, she and Jim had recently bought a condo in Seattle and planned to spend summers there with their relatives. With a big smile, Serena assured Cindy that I was in good hands.

When we were ready to start, I turned to Cindy, "I'll be fine for the next four hours, getting my poison. You don't have to stay."

"Okay, shoot me a text when you're done," she said.

The cancer center was a strange place: it was warm and inviting. The chairs looked like they came from an old ice cream shop in the 1950's. There were patients with all different stages and types of cancer sitting in the chairs. They ranged from the young to the old, and from those who were just skin and bones to those who were full-bodied and healthy-looking.

Serena came over in what she called her "Smurf" suit, which was an extra blue gown over her regular scrubs. She donned latex gloves as well, to keep her safe from the chemicals I was about to get; not the most comforting thought. She used a small needle to inject a numbing agent around my port. It was a small pinch, like getting stung by a bee. Then she connected a needle with a tube through it, like an IV, to my port and, voila, I was hooked up and getting my chemo!

I was about to put on my headphones and turn on my iPad, when the man sitting beside me said, "Howzit, my name is Mikey. Why are you here?"

I put my headphones down and said, "Oh, hi my name is Sarah. I have colon cancer. This is my first day. I have to come here for the next six months. What about you?"

"I got throat cancer. It's my first day too. I have to do chemo, and then I go onto radiation. They say it gets harder after this. I've been eating a lot because they told me that it's going to feel like I have rocks in my throat, and I won't be able to eat much. Pretty much after this, I will be eating and drinking from a straw."

I felt strange listening to him. I still had my hair and appetite, and I started to think about all of the side effects I would experience. None of them seemed as bad as Mikey's and I felt guilty.

From our conversation, I learned that Mikey worked at one of the hotels on the south side of the island. We became chemo buddies and I looked forward to sitting next to him for my next treatment. I joked and said, "Hey, next time save my seat!"

The four hours passed, and Serena returned to unhook the needle from my port and plug me into the portable pump that would be my new companion. As part of my regular treatment, after my four hours of direct chemo, I would be connected to a small pump about the size of a book that continued to deliver additional chemotherapy.

I could walk around while connected to it and carry it in a bag they gave me that resembled a large fanny pack. The pump made a soft clicking sound as the chemo was injected into me. I would be hooked up to it for three days, during which time I could not remove it, even to shower or sleep.

At the end of those three days, I would have to go back to the cancer center so they could remove the pump. I would then have a week and a half off to let my body recover from all the chemo, as they did not want to kill me.

Then I would start the next round with direct chemo first, followed by three days of wearing the pump. I had twelve rounds to do, so I would be at the cancer center twice a month for the next six months. It was April, and September felt far away.

The portable pump made me feel a bit like a robot. My face felt numb and I was unsure if it was a side effect or if it was my nerves. I was not that tired, and I remembered Serena explained that I was also given steroids. As Cindy drove me home, I felt strange and had a bizarre metal sensation flowing through my veins.

When I got home, I called Roland to tell him how everything went. I told him about Serena and how she was from Switzerland. He was busy with work, but wanted to come with me the next time, so he could meet her.

Roland was by my side, when I went back to have my portable pump taken off. Easter was coming up, and the hospital was having a celebration. Serena was dressed up as a bunny rabbit. Her face was painted, she had bunny ears, and a luffa sponge glued to her backside as a tail. With her nose painted black and whiskers on her cheeks, Serena greeted Roland and said, "Gruezi, Mr. Sprecher."

Roland stared back at her decorated whiskers and said, "Hallo."

I was excited that the two of them were meeting. I sat down, and Serena removed the medical tape secured around my port. Then she gently pulled the needle and tube out of my port.

The whole time, she explained in German what she was doing. She looked serious, and I doubt she realized how humorous it was to get medical information from a bunny. Roland listened politely and afterwards laughed and said to me, "That's not what I pictured your Swiss nurse to look like."

chapter 13

EASTER

It was a relief having the pump off. I felt free, it was like taking your shoes and socks off after work and letting your toes wiggle. After my first chemo treatment I was feeling good, though not great. Everything tasted like metal, parts of my hair started falling out, and I noticed that I tired easily. But I was alive.

I followed Dora's food program during chemo, and it was difficult because anything cold gave me a shooting pain in my mouth. As a result, I had to drink what I sarcastically called those "wonderful tasty" green smoothies at room temperature. They were warm and gross, so I tried to drink them in huge gulps.

Dora was my cheerleader, keeping my spirits up by emailing or texting me positive and inspirational quotes. Over the phone Dora told me that getting cancer was my wakeup call in life. It was time for me to start listening and taking care of my body and mind.

She advised me to turn off the television and start the day off by meditating. Clearing my head and working on my breathing techniques would help me through my treatments. If my muscles or stomach was bothering me, Dora suggested that I lay on my left side in bed because it helped with digestion and circulation. Everything she recommended helped and kept me positive.

One evening, I walked Doodle up the street, and I passed by Anne's house. She was in the garage, working on a house project. Buddy ran down the driveway, as we approached. He and Doodle greeted each other with a sniff on the butt. Anne warmly greeted me as well, though without the sniffing. She invited Roland and me to an Easter dinner on Sunday at her house. Thinking of our special diet, I politely declined, but I promised that we would stop by for a drink later in the evening instead.

Around 7:30 on Easter Sunday, Roland and I walked over to Anne's house. There were eight people around the dinner table when we arrived. Anne went into the living room and pulled up two more chairs for us. We were introduced to Bill, Anne's husband. He had a caring personality and a kind smile. Bill was in his sixties and was looking forward to moving to Maui permanently.

It was a fun group of people, and we met some of Anne's friends. I recognized one woman who worked at a local shop, she always wore bright neon clothes, just like my nurse, Serena. It was hard to miss someone with hot pink-framed glasses and a matching neon flower in her hair. Her name was Tammy Lynn, and she had a fun-loving personality to match her bold style.

Bill gave Roland and I, the tour of the "new" house. He took us upstairs and there was an unobstructed view of the volcano from their back window. From their bedroom, they had built a lanai in the front of the house. We stood out on the balcony and there was a clear view of the ocean and the West Maui Mountains.

After the tour of the house, we joined the dinner party. Bill took a seat next to Roland and asked, "So, I can hear an accent, where are you from?"

"Switzerland," Roland said.

"Well, I have to ask. Why the hell is a Swiss guy in Hawaii wearing a Toledo Mud Hens shirt?" Bill was baffled and laughed at the question.

I laughed and said, "Oh, I'm from Toledo, Ohio and my brother bought the shirt for Roland as a gift."

Bill was a baseball fan and loved the Boston Red Sox's. He and Roland started talking about baseball teams and stats. I had been hoping that we arrived late enough, and that dinner would be over, but I was wrong. Anne had finished cooking, and everyone started to eat.

We stayed while everyone ate and after dinner Anne came and sat next to me. "Thanks for coming tonight. It's really great to see you. Did you start your chemotherapy yet?"

"I had my first treatment last week. It went really well; I've got more energy than I thought I would. I don't know if it's from the steroids they give, but I'm staying positive."

She put her hand on my shoulder and said, "I'm glad to hear that Sarah. If you need any help with Doodle or anything, just call or come over."

Her kindness and care meant a lot to me and I appreciated all of her advice. I smiled and hugged my new friend and said, "Thanks Anne, I'm really happy we met."

chapter 14

IS YOUR FACEMASK ON?

Time flew by, and my second treatment was coming up. I was in an upbeat mood when Cindy picked me up for my appointment. I was keeping myself busy by planning my birthday party for the following week. Cindy loved planning parties, so we chatted away about the guest list and food, as we headed towards the clinic.

I looked over at Cindy at one point as she drove and noticed that she was rather pale. Worried, I said, "Are you okay?"

"I was feeling better until this morning, I'm just a little nauseous."

"Well, you should go to the doctor."

She was not in the mood for a lecture. "I'm getting my colonoscopy in a week, aren't I?"

"Look, I'm getting the chemo and I'm the one worried about you."

I could tell she was tired and with a hint of sarcasm she said, "Whatever, Mom."

Walking into the cancer center, I saw that Mikey was already hooked up, so I picked the seat beside his. I was stunned by his appearance. He looked like he had lost about twenty pounds over the past two weeks. He could hardly talk and couldn't eat at all because of the pain. He didn't even want to drink out of a straw, though he knew he had to.

I looked pretty much the same, just with thinner hair, but Mikey's drastic change in appearance, hit me hard emotionally. Cancer doesn't have one universal "look" and I tried to imagine all the pain he must be in. He was tired and closed his eyes and fell asleep. I picked up my bag and moved seats. I didn't want to bother him or interrupt his sleep.

After seeing Mikey, my mood was somber, and I patiently waited for Serena. She walked over to me and she had purple glitter eye shadow on and greeted me with a big smile and said, "Hello my darling! I'm happy to see my Swiss miss!"

My face lit up and her positive energy lifted my spirits. She was already in her "smurf" suit and she started to hook me up to the chemo. "How did you do your first week?" she asked.

"I feel good, I'm on this new 'green' diet and started meditating."

She stuck her hand up for a high five and said, "You go girl! I'm impressed. Were you always a vegetarian?"

I lightly slapped her latex glove. "Oh no, this is all new since my diagnosis."

"I think it's awesome. Chemotherapy, with the advances in medical technology has made leaps and bounds in the past decade with treating cancer but I also believe in healing the whole body, mind and spirit. May I ask, how you came upon your new diet?"

"My husband and a friend have been helping me."

"You're very lucky to have people supporting you along this journey. I am a vegetarian and I listen to daily affirmations as they inspire gratitude and love. It's so wonderful to learn about you making all these positive changes."

I looked up at Serena and thought, *How did the stars align for us to meet?* The strange coincidence that she was Swiss and understood my diet and new path in life, were incredible to me.

Cindy picked me up, looking tired and still not feeling well. We did not talk much on the ride home, as this time I was worn-out. It was strange the both of us, so quiet in the car.

I called Cindy the next morning at 6:30, as I always did, and it went to her voicemail. *She is probably taking a shower*, I thought, as I started the coffee pot. The phone rang an hour later, and the caller ID identified it as Cindy.

I picked up, but it was not Cindy on the other end of the line, it was Jim. "Cindy wasn't feeling that great this morning and she went to the ER. They are going to do an emergency surgery on her."

I almost spilled my coffee and said, "What? What are you talking about?"

Jim's voice shook as he answered, "She has a tumor in her colon. It could rupture and kill her."

"I'm leaving my house now and I'll be there, as soon as I can."

I grabbed my keys and hurried to the car. As I got in, I heard the *Click!* of my pump; there went more chemo into my system. *Shit!* I thought, remembering that I was not supposed to be exposed to sick people because my immune system was compromised. I ran back inside the house and grabbed a surgical facemask from the box it was in. I had bought them a month earlier, after my first meeting with the nurse.

I raced to the emergency room, facemask on and chemo bag in hand. I asked where Cindy was, and a nurse led me into the ER through the double doors. Jim was standing in the hallway. "Cindy was wheeled up to surgery five minutes ago."

I had missed her by minutes and was talking too loud for the ER. I shouted to Jim, "What happened?"

Before he could respond, a nurse came by and asked me about my mask. I looked at her and said, "I'm getting my chemotherapy."

"You know you shouldn't be here of all places," she said. I knew that and was questioning was this really happening. What in the world was happening?

In the evening, Roland and I went to see Cindy at the hospital. My facemask was back on as we entered through the glass door. We both knew it all too well: it was the same hospital I had been in three months before. I saw the same nurses and ran into the travelling nurse from Kentucky. "What are you doing here?" she asked.

"I'm visiting a friend."

She took my arm to stop me and excitedly confided, "I found someone that looks at me the way your husband looks at you."

She had met an amazing man at some event and was head-over-heels in love. Now she was looking for a full-time position at the hospital and planned on moving to Maui for good so they could be together. Her story briefly distracted me from the chaos that surrounded me, and I congratulated her.

Cindy's room was a few doors down from my old room. She was asleep and hooked up to all the familiar machines when Roland and I walked in. Jim told us Cindy's diagnosis; she had colon cancer and the surgeon had to take out half of her colon. She had stage 3 colon cancer and would need six months of the same chemotherapy that I was getting, and then eight weeks of radiation after that.

Am I going crazy? I asked myself. *This can't be real.*

Cindy started to wake up from her drugged-up state and looked at Roland on one side of her bed, and then me, on the other. Confused and dazed she muttered a few words and then in classic Cindy style said, "Fuck a duck."

We sat in silence, each of us holding one of her hands. Through my facemask I said, "We are going to beat this together, Cindy."

We sat quiet in the room for a moment and the click of my chemotherapy pump was all we heard.

chapter 15

THE BIRTHDAY PARTY

We were all in shock. How could Cindy have colon cancer? I remembered her stupid joke, about having the same thing I had while I was in the hospital. Was this some kind of sick joke the universe was playing on us? I thought about what Emalia had said to me at the park, "What surprises life gives you."

Not all surprises are good. I was angry. *Why did cancer exist? Why did Cindy have to go through this too? Why did Emalia have to die? Why were all these bad things happening to me? Why me!*

My phone beeped, and I saw that I had a text message. It was from Dora. I clicked on the screen and saw her message. It was one of the many inspirational quotes she had sent, and it read, "Your illness does not define you. Your strength and courage do."

I knew I needed to stay positive, not only for myself but for Cindy also. I had to overcome my negative thoughts, and I would not allow myself to fall into despair. I took a deep breath, and I felt the stress and anger start to leave my body.

I wasn't supposed to be exposed to sick people, but I still visited Cindy every day. She was pale and tired, and always greeted me with a weak, "Hey kiddo."

At one point, she said, "I don't think I'm going to be able to make it to your birthday party."

"It's okay, Cindy. You'll make it to my next one."

It was already May and I was about to turn thirty-eight. I thought about Emalia a lot, and how lucky I was to be turning another year older. My past birthdays were never that important to me, but now things were different.

Through Facebook friends, I found the site dedicated to Emalia. It contained her obituary and photos from her life. She was forty-two years old when she died. Active and fit, she looked like the epitome of health in all the pictures. I still couldn't wrap my mind around how she of all people got colon cancer. In a sense, I was asking the same question about myself.

As I scrolled through the site, there was a message that talked about Emalia and her spirit. In the Native Hawaiian culture, they believe in Aumakuas, ancestors who have passed away that are transformed into family gods. They watch over their living descendants and act as protectors or guardians. It stated that Emalia had come back to her family as an owl. It created a beautiful image to me that she was still watching over her loved ones.

Staring at the pictures of her on my computer screen, I saw a beaming young woman whose life was tragically cut short. You could see that she had a beautiful life filled with love from family and friends. I sat and stared at that page for many nights and cried. I cried for her, and I cried because I didn't want to die as well.

We had planned a big celebration for my birthday party and invited around thirty people. My friends Julie and Grace helped with the decorations and brought the cake.

Cindy was stuck in the hospital and would indeed miss the party, as she predicted. I was running errands when she called to tell me that Jim would drop my birthday card off at the house. She had bought it before she got sick. "Thanks, Cindy. I will call you in the morning and tell you how it all turns out."

Cindy's birthday card was wedged in the front door. I sat down and opened the envelope. On the front of the card was Winnie-the-Pooh sitting arm-in-arm with Piglet on a log. It read, "*We'll be friends forever. Maybe even longer.* Happy Birthday, signed Cindy and Jim." I smiled and wondered, *after everything that had occurred in the past week, how in the world did Cindy end up picking out the perfect card?*

Guests began to arrive, and my house started to fill with people. Everyone was talking and laughing. It was a magnificent sight to see all of my friends together. My birthday cake was brought out and the singing began. Smiling, I blew out my candles. I didn't wish for a thing because being alive was enough of a gift. The night was filled with love and laugher. I looked at Roland and he lifted me up and kissed me in front of everyone.

chapter 16

THIRD TIME'S A CHARM

I t was time for my third treatment, and now I had to drive myself. I gathered my water bottles, iPad, and snacks and got in the car. It was strange driving without Cindy.

I knew it was Mikey's last treatment, but I didn't see him, and I assumed he must have had a different time slot this week. There was a seat in the corner that I picked, and Serena greeted me with her usual smile. "Hello darling, I'm so sorry I missed taking your pump out last week. I caught a really bad cold and of course, I don't want to get any of my beautiful patients sick. Where is Cindy today?"

"You won't believe this, but Cindy had emergency surgery last week and has colon cancer. She is supposed to get the same treatment as me."

For a brief moment, she was speechless. "Sarah, I'm so sorry for you and for Cindy. How devastating this all must be for you."

"I know, it's all a little overwhelming. Do you think you can help her too?

"Of course, Sarah. I will do everything in my power to make sure I'm assigned to Cindy when she is ready for her treatment. Please let her know I am sending my best wishes and prayers to her as she heals."

"Thank you, Serena, for everything."

The third treatment hit me harder than the first two. My breathing was heavy, and I had little energy and strength. By the time I came back three days later to have my pump taken off, my body was exhausted. I left the cancer center and walked across the hallway through the hospital and took the elevator up to see Cindy.

My facemask firmly on, I knocked on Cindy's door. She wound up getting a bad infection and I saw she was getting a blood transfusion. Her surgery was more invasive than mine. Cindy had been in the hospital for over two weeks and was becoming depressed. She wanted to go home.

She started telling me about her surgeon. He lived up the street from her. Cindy being Cindy, would often yell at him to slow down as he drove past her house in his truck. I laughed and said, "Well, at least if you have any problems, you know where he lives."

We started comparing notes on the nurses and our scars. Cindy said, "You didn't have to stay in the hospital this long."

"Well, you got to eat food and didn't have a tube shoved down your throat."

She was upset that they had to take out half of her colon and could not do the laparoscopic surgery they did with me, leaving her with a big scar down her belly. I lifted up my shirt to show her my scars. She took one look at my small incisions and said, "No fair. My scar looks like a giant centipede."

Trying to cheer her up, I said, "Well, you're going to be out of the hospital in no time and I talked to Serena about being your nurse too."

"Oh Serena, what a wonderful young woman she is."

I got home from the hospital after lunchtime and Roland called from work. He was getting a pain in his side and was panic stricken. "Could it be cancer?" he asked.

"Roland, cancer isn't contagious. You're being ridiculous."

He was genuinely freaking out, so I promised to call the doctor and make an appointment for him. The earliest appointment they had would be in a week, and a CAT scan in a month. I called Roland to let him know and he was upset with the news. "I can't wait that long."

"Well, the only other option is to go to the ER. They can do a CAT scan right then and there." This, I knew from personal experience.

He thought it over for a moment, "Okay, I'm leaving work and will drive straight to the hospital."

I got in my car and drove back to the hospital. The ER was busy, and we had to wait a long time, as Roland was not a high priority emergency. I had my facemask on, and people were coughing all around us.

As we sat in the waiting room, I thought about what Dora had once said over the phone about Roland. "Sarah, you are married to a special man. Not all men are as sensitive and loving as Roland. Some men close off their feelings when their wives get sick. I can only hope that one day, my daughter meets someone as sweet as Roland."

Roland had bags under his eyes and was worried. The last few months, he was dealing with me, work, and now Cindy. It took a tremendous toll on him and I felt guilty. I did not realize how stressful everything was for him. For the first time, I tried to put myself in his shoes. I realized that if he had cancer and might die, I would have gone completely crazy.

When we got to see a doctor, it was the same one that had stuck his finger up my rear end and sent me home. Through his glasses, he said to Roland, "You're a healthy young man. It's probably a torn or over-stretched muscle."

I looked up at him defiantly and said, "Well, you told me I was constipated, and it turned out that I actually had colon cancer."

After hearing that, the doctor ordered a CAT scan and blood tests. I put my hand on Roland's face, "Honey, you're going to be fine. The tests are going to come back clean and you can be free of worry."

He looked uncomfortable and rubbed his stomach. They rolled him away for his CAT scan, and I was left alone to wait. *Now I know how he must have felt,* I thought. Waiting for the results from the scan was stressful, but when they came back saying that Roland was fine, his sigh of relief was worth it.

We got home around dinnertime, and a shooting pain stabbed through my stomach as we walked in the door. It felt like razor blades were cutting through my intestines, and I started throwing up. We turned around and drove back to the ER, the nurse checking us in said, "Weren't you already here today?"

"Yes, but for my husband. I'm in a lot of pain right now. I'm getting chemotherapy at the moment and I don't know if this is a bad side effect."

I did not have to sit in the waiting room this time, and they brought me straight into a room. The nurses hooked me up to an IV to get fluids and gave me painkillers. The morphine did the job and the pain went away. The doctors didn't know if I had a reaction to the chemotherapy or if the stress of the day triggered the pain.

They released me from the ER and after the third trip to the hospital, my bed felt like heaven. We were both exhausted from the day and Roland held me close, as I fell asleep in his arms.

chapter 17

OUR SERENA

One afternoon, I walked Doodle up the street and saw Anne walking up her driveway. She invited me in the house, and we left Buddy and Doodle in the yard. She started to pick up things around the house and said, "I've got so much packing to do. Bill and I are going to spend the summer on the mainland. My daughter is getting married and then we are going to spend the rest of the time visiting family and friends.

"Wow, that sounds like an amazing summer. When will you be back?"

"We are coming back in the fall sometime. My mother is coming back with us and I have to get her settled and pack all of her things too. So, lots of planning but enough about me. How are you doing with your chemotherapy?"

I proudly told her I was doing okay with the treatments and had high hopes. I didn't get the response I thought I would. Anne seemed a little nervous and cautioned me. "It's only been two months; your body will get weaker as time goes on."

I was slightly hurt by the comment because I expected a pat on the back. She saw the disappointment in my face and then added with a mischievous grin, "Hey, I'm sure you will do great, and look at me! I'm living proof that only the good die young."

I laughed, and realized I was a little sad that she was leaving for so long, as I enjoyed her company. I could see that she was extremely busy and so I excused myself. As we headed toward the front door, I said, "Well, hopefully you'll be back before Halloween. My friend does a huge haunted house for Halloween. I would love to take you to see it."

"That sounds great. Halloween is my favorite holiday. I love all the parties and wearing crazy costumes. I will look forward to seeing the haunted house. So, I guess this is goodbye, good luck with your chemo and take care of yourself."

I hugged Anne goodbye and said, "I hope you have a great summer and I'll see you in a few months."

Cindy had finally been released from the hospital, and now it was her turn to meet with the oncologist and nurse at the cancer clinic. Living on an island with one hospital, it was no surprise that Cindy ended up with the same doctor. Serena kept her promise and Cindy was assigned to her; she now was "our" Serena.

Thankfully, the following rounds of treatment went smoothly with no unwanted surprises. Summer came and I was more than halfway through my chemo, and Cindy was just beginning hers.

We only had one treatment at the cancer center together. I assumed the reason was because we annoyed everyone with our non-stop chatter and laughter. We were like hens clucking all day. After the one treatment together, the clerk scheduled us to go on different days.

It was a surreal time. Cindy and I talked every morning at 6:30 and we traded stories about our symptoms. My feet tingled from the cold, and Cindy complained about the awful metallic taste in her mouth.

We talked about our chemo bags. I wore mine around my waist like a fanny pack, while Cindy preferred to carry hers like a purse. I would go over to Cindy's house after my treatments, and she would make eggs and cut up fresh fruit for me. We gossiped away like little schoolgirls as she boiled water for our afternoon tea.

We were also learning more about our nurse, Serena. Serena was like Tinker Bell, spreading her fairy dust around the cancer center. She would give special blue ribbons that had, "Who I Am Makes A Difference," on them, and affirmation cards that read, "The world needs more people like you," to her patients and their friends.

Serena was studying Reiki, training for half marathons and fun runs. She loved sunset cruises and long walks on the beach and was single. Cindy and I secretly made plans to find a man for "our" Serena.

"Sarah, I think the world of Serena. She shouldn't be single," Cindy said to me one day as we were commiserating. I was already on the same page and heartily agreed. Let the matchmaking begin!

Cindy ran through the short list, of all the single men, she knew and said, "There is a cute guy from the hardware store, who helped me the other day, and he looked to be around Serena's age."

"Most of the people you mentioned are strangers you met at the store. How do you know that guy doesn't have a girlfriend already? He could be married for all you know!"

"Well, you do have a point there," she said.

Doubtful she could find a suitable suitor, I said, "Let me deal with the matchmaking."

I asked Serena how she felt about getting matched up with someone and she was open to the idea.

I had one man in mind for Serena. His name was Dan and he occasionally worked with Roland. I had met him at a Christmas work party a few years back and seen him at other work gatherings. I did not know him very well, but Roland told me he had recently broken up with his girlfriend.

I set up a double dinner date with Serena and Dan at a touristy Mexican restaurant. I was excited on the drive over and laid out my whole plan for the evening to Roland. If they hit it off, we would make up an excuse to leave early and let them continue the night together alone.

Serena was already waiting at a table when we arrived. She was wearing a colorful flower print dress with long feather earrings. Dan entered the restaurant, looking clean cut in a buttoned-down shirt. I introduced them and he was shy and polite. They started off asking the typical first-date questions and I was thrilled to see some chemistry between them.

When Serena excused herself to go to the restroom, I followed. I was like a little girl, excited to find out what she thought of Dan. I grabbed her hand and she squeezed it in return. "He's really cute!" she said.

Roland was quite chatty all night, and I had to kick him under the table a few times to allow Serena and Dan to talk with each other. I began to initiate my exit plan. "Roland is so busy with work; he has to wake up very early tomorrow morning. We had better leave."

"I'm not that busy. I don't have to get up early." Roland said.

I shot him a look and interrupted, "Yes, you do. Don't you remember on the drive over? You told me; you had a busy day tomorrow."

I kicked him again under the table, "Oh, I guess I'm really busy tomorrow. We had better get going."

Roland and I hurried out of the restaurant and gave the new couple an awkward rushed goodbye. When we got in the car, I raised my voice and said, "Hello?! Didn't you hear the exit plan before we got there?"

I was ecstatic that Serena and Dan seemed to hit it off. When we got home, I sent Cindy a text about the date. Later that night, my phone beeped, and I saw Serena had texted me. I looked at the screen and read, "We had a walk along the beach after you left."

I was dying to know more and instantly wrote back, "Did you kiss?"

She replied with a few emojis, followed by a "Yes!"

I was over the moon and went to bed excited for Serena.

The new blooming romance was all Cindy, Serena, and I could talk about at the cancer center. Cindy and I listened intently as Serena told us about their dates and how much she liked him. I, of course, got to gloat to Cindy about being the perfect matchmaker. She joked that I ought to start a new business.

chapter 18

LOVE IS IN THE AIR

t was August 1st, and before I had met Roland, the day meant nothing to me. As Roland's wife, I learned that it was Switzerland's Independence Day. Surprisingly, there were quite a few Swiss people living on the island and there was even a Swiss restaurant on Maui. Every year, the restaurant had a special party to celebrate the holiday with a buffet featuring traditional Swiss delicacies and there was live music. It was a festive atmosphere and the singer yodeled and played the accordion.

Before Roland, the only Swiss foods I knew of were the cheese and the chocolate. On our trips to Switzerland, Roland introduced me to the different foods there, including the ever-popular cheese and meat fondue. The Swiss cuisine was delicious, and I loved the homemade sausages, wiener schnitzel, pastas rich with cheese and decadent pastries.

With our new diet, we hardly ate at the Swiss restaurant, but we decided this year's August 1st celebration was special. We would have to avoid all the meat and heavy pastas, but the restaurant had salads for us to eat. I invited Serena and Dan to join us. Cindy was coping with the chemo well and she and Jim wanted to come too.

Cindy was excited to be out and about. She had a wig on, to cover her thinning hair and wore a tee shirt from Switzerland that Roland had given her. Her lipstick and blush covered her pale skin and she was wearing gold earrings and a necklace.

My hair was also thin and patchy from the treatments, but I wore baseball caps and beanies instead of a wig. I never wore makeup and I didn't own any jewelry; I was still a tomboy.

It was a fun evening. Cindy held Jim close, and I watched Serena and Dan hold hands. All of us were full of the delicious food and sang as the band played the music. We celebrated and yodeled the night away.

Our ten-year wedding anniversary was coming up and we were planning on celebrating as we did every year: at a well-known restaurant called Mama's Fish House. It was located next to a small beach and there was a view of the ocean from every table. The restaurant was full of beautiful exotic flower arrangements, and the menu offered superb fish dishes that were as fresh as you could get.

The night of our anniversary we went to Mama's and we were waiting to be seated. I held Roland's hand and could not believe how fast the ten years had passed. Roland leaned in for a kiss and said, "You look so beautiful."

The way he looked at me gave me a quiet confidence and made me feel special. Even though I was not the "typical" woman, Roland only had eyes for me. I didn't own a dress, fancy shoes or a purse. I wore jeans, or khaki shorts, flip-flops and kept my wallet and phone in my pocket.

When the hostess called out, "Sprecher, party of two." I smiled and remembered my mother demanding that I take Roland's surname after we were married. I was independent and liked my maiden name but in the end my mother won. I was glad I took it, and my different name symbolized my new life with Roland.

We were seated and Roland ordered his usual mai tai. I asked him to hold his drink up and snapped a photo. I looked at my camera and saw the lighting hid the patches of hair missing on his five 'o clock shadow. The past year was rough, and my cancer diagnosis put a strain on him. Signs of his stress started to show up. He started to develop alopecia on his face and as his beard grew in, there were tiny areas where the hair stopped growing.

Sadly, Roland dealt with the stress of illness and death before. His parents, both were deceased. We rarely spoke of them, as they passed away before we had met. His mother took her own life when he was four years old, and when Roland was twenty-one years old, his father died of ALS, also known as Lou Gehrig's disease.

We ordered dinner and I touched Roland's hand on the table. I felt as though we were two orphans, who were lucky to have found each other.

September arrived and I was almost done with my chemotherapy treatment. It was a strange feeling: I was so happy that it was going to be over, but I was going to miss seeing all of the caring staff and people at the cancer center.

I never did get to see Mikey again, and hoped that I would eventually run into him, as Maui was a small island. Chemotherapy was a giant part of my life for the past six months and it was coming to an end. On my last day, Serena greeted me with a hug and said, "Girl, congratulations! You did great! You're an inspiration to us all!"

"Thanks Serena, I couldn't imagine going through it without you."

She disconnected my portable pump and took the cartridge of chemo out of the bag and asked, "Do you want to keep your chemo bag? I have a lot of patients that keep them as a reminder of their journey."

"I guess I will keep it, but I'm a little freaked out by all of the chemicals it's been exposed to. I don't think I want it in my house. Can I burn it instead?"

I was laughing at the question. Serena with a wide-open mouth said, "Oh my gosh, that is an awesome idea!"

Cindy stopped by the center to support me on my last day. When she heard that I was planning on burning my bag she said, "I want to burn mine too."

The three of us decided to have a bag-burning beach party once Cindy finished her chemo and radiation treatments. My doctor walked in the room and gave me the results of my latest CAT scan and blood work. He looked down at his chart and said, "No signs of cancer."

Immediately, I called Roland and told him the good news. Tears rolled down my face and I said, "I'm cancer free!"

chapter 19

BEND

I t was possible for the cancer to return, and the doctor advised me to keep my port in for one year, in case there was a reoccurrence. I scheduled monthly appointments at the cancer center to get my port flushed. They had to inject a saline solution through the port so blood clots wouldn't form. While in remission, I would continue to be monitored with blood tests, CAT scans and checkups.

I was on an extended medical leave from work. It turned out, that I had neuropathy, which was nerve damage in my limbs that caused numbness and pain. There were times when I could not feel my feet and I had to watch every step to avoid falling or twisting my ankle. The doctor said it might go away, or I might have it the rest of my life. It was collateral damage from my treatment.

Cindy suggested that Roland and I should use her timeshare in Bend, Oregon to celebrate the completion of my treatment. Since she and Jim weren't going anywhere this year, it seemed perfect that Roland and I go. "The leaves will be changing color in the mountains, and it is beautiful," she said.

I had never been to Bend Oregon but had heard many stories about it from Cindy. It was where she and Jim first met. They both were attending some convention there and whenever Cindy told the story of their first meeting, Jim always chimed in and said, "It was the good old days of skiing all day and partying all night."

The rest was history. We eagerly agreed to Cindy and Jim's gift, and we were looking forward to a getaway.

Bend, Oregon was as beautiful as Cindy described it, and the timeshare was elegant and fancy. The living room had stunning views and a fireplace, and the kitchen was huge and modern. The bathroom was tiled with Italian travertine and in the bedroom, there was a four-poster bed. It had Cindy's taste and style written all over it.

I looked out the window and there was a large maple tree where the leaves had turned a golden yellow in front of the lake. The mountains were behind the shimmering lake and it was a picture-perfect view.

It was the first time I had been somewhere cold since my chemotherapy started and my feet tingled in my shoes. I found the neuropathy was more noticeable when

I was cold or when my feet were constricted in shoes or socks. It made me thankful to live in a warm climate, where I pretty much always wore flip-flops.

It was a romantic week for Roland and me. I called Cindy every day to give her full updates on what we were doing. I could hear the excitement in her voice and in a sense, she was living vicariously through us. "Did you drive around the lake and check out the shops at the sun river village? I know you hate to shop, but it has some great restaurants. You should eat there tonight," she said over the phone.

"We are planning on driving around the mountains and stopping at Benham Falls Trail."

"Oh, Sarah it's such a gorgeous view, you will love the hike down to the waterfall."

Roland and I arrived at the park and found a parking stall next to the trailhead. We started hiking down the path and I tried to imagine Cindy's old life here. I pictured her all dolled up in a ski outfit going down the mountain slopes in the wintertime.

At her house on Maui, I had seen an old photo of her wearing a fur coat and holding a glass of champagne with long blond hair. I only knew her as a brunette and she had kept her hair on the shorter side now. I pictured her laughing at fancy black tie events and the one thing I knew for sure about Cindy, was that she knew how to have a good time.

Cindy was happy that we were enjoying her old stomping grounds but at times I could hear a certain melancholy tone in her voice. I worried about her a lot. I knew the chemotherapy was harder on her than it was for me.

Roland and I made it to the end of the trail, and it opened up to a beautiful waterfall. We sat down on a rock and took out some snacks to eat. I was in awe of the beauty and could feel the power of the waterfall and I thought of Cindy. How, in a strange cosmic way, having the same cancer together, at the same time, was a godsend for the both of us. The cancer created a special bond between us, and it could never be broken.

chapter 20

It Takes A Village

D ora was staying at her condo on Maui for a few weeks, and I was excited to finally meet her in person. We met for dinner and she greeted Roland with a big hug. I was surprised to see how tiny and petite she was. She took her hands to my face and said, "Sarah, look at you, you're beautiful."

We sat down for dinner and Dora had a lot to say and a lot of things going on in her life. It was as if she knew how short life was and wanted to make sure she didn't miss a thing. She told us about her husband and daughter and whipped out her phone to show us pictures of her dog.

With an intense passion, Dora started to spout off new health revelations. She talked about genetic predisposition, probiotics in the stomach, and the importance of breast milk to the overall immune system. She said, "Sarah, we have all of the tools that we need to be healthy, we just have to start listening to our bodies."

"Thanks, Dora, for everything. Your diet and guidance really helped me during my chemotherapy. Now that it's over, I'm a little anxious and worried about what I'm supposed to do next.

"Sarah be good to yourself. Try not to get stressed out because stress can weaken the immune system and create an unhealthy body. So, make sure you continue meditating and take some time for yourself during the day. Maybe, try doing yoga."

"I'm not really the yoga type of person. I haven't meditated for a while. I know I should. I get busy and it's hard for me to slow down."

She started to shake her head, "No excuses, Sarah. Meditation helps you clear your mind of negative thoughts. Try to live with intention and meaning."

"I know, I promise I will try to take the time to do it."

Dora took my hand and looked me in the eyes. "Sarah, getting cancer is going to be one of the best things that could have happened to you, because now you are going to live a healthier and happier life."

One afternoon my friend, Grace stopped by the house after her shift at the airport. She was like the sister I never had. Grace was from the Midwest and moved to Maui after college. She was married with kids and Roland and I were always invited to celebrate the holidays with her family. We talked to each other on the phone regularly and she kept me updated on all the news at work.

Grace came in the front door and sat down on the couch. She nonchalantly asked, "So now that you're done with chemo and you don't have to go back to work, what are you going to do with all of your free time?"

My face went blank and I was speechless. It was a simple question but the weight of it felt so heavy. I literally had no idea what I wanted to do, and it occurred to me that somewhere along the line, I had lost my self-identity. I felt tears spring to my eyes as I considered this. I had gone through a life-altering trauma and survived. For more than six months cancer defined me. Now that it was over, who was I?

I had put on a brave face since my diagnosis and I could not stay strong in that moment and the tears started falling. There was a feeling of hopelessness and I couldn't stop crying. "I don't know, Grace. I feel sick inside and I'm scared of everything. I worry about everyone and everything. I don't know what I'm supposed to do. I really don't know who I am anymore."

Grace moved over and hugged me, but I couldn't stop crying. I was getting choked up and as I wiped my face I said, "I just survived cancer and should be happy. So why do I feel this way? Why am I like this? What's wrong with me?"

There was no exact pinpoint of time when my fears and anxieties took control of my life. The years and the day-to-day busy-ness of life took over, and after a while, I stopped doing things that I used to love because I was too afraid.

I would watch the news or hear about a tragedy and worry it could happen to me. I became fearful of things that in my youth were of no consequence. The free-spirited girl that drove to Alaska and ended up in Hawaii had vanished.

Grace comforted me and held my shoulders and looked me straight in the eyes and said, "Sarah, you are a strong courageous woman. You went through hell and now we're going to get you all better. We will find what makes you happy. Didn't you used to surf, Why don't you start again?"

I looked down at the ground and said, "I haven't been in the ocean for years. I'm terrified of sharks. I'm scared of drowning. What if something bad happens?"

Grace said, "I started stand-up-paddling and the cool thing is you're not sitting in the water completely since you're standing on the board."

I looked up at her and could see she had made up her mind. "Sarah you are going to be my paddling partner and I'm going to help you get back in the water."

I hugged her tightly and through my tears agreed to be her surf buddy.

The next day I called my friend Julie. Julie was my partner-in-crime and we hung out together all the time. I loved how different we were from each other. We were complete opposites. I was serious and would get stressed out easily. Julie on the other hand, was carefree and she laughed at everything. I hated scary shows and she loved horror movies. I ate the same food all of the time and Julie tried every new snack or drink that came out. Her house was filled from top to bottom with pictures and memorabilia from her life and my house was bare and nothing hung on the walls.

Despite our personality differences, our friendship worked. Julie answered the phone, "Hey Sarah, what's up?"

"I'm going to learn how-to stand-up paddle and I need to buy a new bathing suit. You want to come to the store with me?"

Julie started laughing, "What!? That's a great idea. I've known you for seven years and I've never seen you at the beach or in a bathing suit."

"I know it's been a long time since I've been in the ocean," I said.

"Well, if you're going to stand up paddle, I'm bringing my surfboard and coming with you!"

With the encouragement of my friends, I made up my mind and I was going to go back into the ocean. I asked

Roland to help me get over my fear. When he got home from work, we went to the beach. I was nervous about getting in the water and Roland held my hand. I took tiny baby steps into the ocean and felt the warm water on my skin. Anxious thoughts of sharks circling and looking to bite off my toes started to creep into my mind. I pushed the idea out of my head and instead thought of all my friends supporting me. I got in and dunked my head underwater.

Roland and I went to the beach every day for two weeks straight and each day got a little bit better. The thoughts of sharks started to subside, and I was more comfortable in the water. I told myself, *I can do this.*

chapter 21

HALLOWEEN

Roland and I had never been big on celebrating holidays until we met Julie and her husband Harvey. No holiday was too small for them and they celebrated each one with over-the-top flair. Julie would squeal with delight talking about them and Harvey always said, "Holidays are a reason to have an awesome party."

It was Halloween and we were summoned by Julie and Harvey to help at their house. Every year, they put together a huge haunted house for Halloween. It would take Harvey a whole week to set everything up.

He had been collecting Halloween items from the Salvation Army, Goodwill, and various hardware stores for more than twenty years, and as a result, he had just about every spooky accessory one could imagine. It grew so large, that they recruited helpers to scare the neighborhood children. It was almost too scary for many of the kids, and even some of the parents, to enter the haunted house.

In the past, Roland had worn a hockey mask and charged at the kids with a fake chainsaw, and he couldn't wait to scare the kids again this year. My duty was to dress up as a scary clown and sit inside the haunted house and direct the children on where to go next.

I sat in the semi-dark room with a bucket of candy, waiting for the kids, as the scary music blared, and the black lights flickered. Julie was outside near the front of the house, dressed up as a witch, shrieking into the microphone, "Come, come to the haunted house, if you dare!"

I had told Cindy about the haunted house years ago, but she never made it over to see it before. This year, she mustered the energy to drive over with Jim. My phone beeped with a text from Cindy. They had arrived and I left my post and set the bucket of candy on the chair. I made my way through the maze of darkness and saw Cindy and Jim waiting outside the driveway.

I took my clown mask off and said, "Cindy you made it! How are you feeling?"

"Like shit, but never mind me, this is terrific!"

"Hold my hand and I will give you the grand tour."

"Let me put my facemask on first. This will make me look pretty scary." She said, as she reached into her purse and put her surgical mask on.

We walked through the haunted house and Cindy loved all of the decorations and laughed when she heard Julie over the speakers, talking on the microphone, trying to frighten the kids. When we reached the end, Roland popped out and scared Cindy with his chainsaw. Cindy let out a delightful laugh and said, "Thanks for getting me out of the house for this. It's better than I could have ever imagined."

Cindy was tired from the chemotherapy, so she and Jim didn't stay very long. I hugged her goodbye and enjoyed the rest of the evening. It was getting late, and the kids stopped trick-or-treating, and we helped clean up.

I thought about our neighbors, Anne and Bill, as I picked up candy wrappers off the ground. Earlier that day, I had walked up the street to see if they were back on the island yet. The house was still empty, and I tried calling Anne, but it went to voicemail. I didn't leave a message because I didn't want to bother her while she was spending time with her family.

I wondered when she was coming home, but I figured I would see her eventually when she got back to Maui. I looked up at the Halloween decorations and laughed at how outrageous the haunted house was. I was definitely going to have Anne come next year.

chapter 22

CLASSMATES

I visited Cindy during her treatments, and we were constantly comparing our experiences. My veins were small, and I had painful memories of the nurses pricking me with the needles trying to find a vein for my IV. The nurses didn't have any problems finding Cindy's "porno veins," as she called them. Her veins were large and stuck out.

Our ports were also different from each other. My port was small and hardly poked out of my body, while Cindy had a different brand and it was much larger than mine. Her port had a giant nob and stuck out noticeably. She said, "Look at my port, it's huge compared to yours."

I laughed and joked, "That's what you get for scolding your doctor. I bet you'll think twice about yelling at him the next time you see him driving down the hill."

We also had many of the same problems with our treatment. At different times each of us had our treatments postponed due to low white blood cell counts, which extended the treatment time. When it happened to me, I took it in stride. When it happened to Cindy, she was boiling mad. I tried to explain to her that there was nothing she could do but she was too angry to listen to reason.

Like kids in school we were always comparing ourselves to each other. Cindy had to go to another island to get a special scan, called a PET scan. She asked our doctor, "Why do I have to go? Sarah didn't have to go."

"Well, you're not Sarah, are you?" he said.

I then had to ask our doctor, "Why did I not get a PET scan?"

"You're not Cindy," he said.

Everyone loved Cindy at the cancer center; her charisma charmed the whole staff. I connected with Serena, but I didn't know much about the other nurses. Cindy knew the life stories of all of the nurses and doctors. I listened to her chat about the doctor and I said, "Tell a phone, tell a friend, tell a Cindy."

The chemotherapy took its toll on Cindy and she had a lot more nausea and pain then I did. She started smoking pot to manage her symptoms. She didn't believe in the "Dora diet" the way Roland and I did. So, I had my green smoothies and she had her marijuana.

Even with all the pot smoking, she was still suffering physically and frustrated that she couldn't do the things she wanted. Cindy wanted her freedom back; she was tired of being sick. The chemo treatments made her feel awful most of the time, and I understood how deeply she missed her old life.

She did have positive outlets to relive her stress. The manicurist Cindy went to, loved her so much that she made special house calls for her. Cindy received her facials and manicures from home.

Her dog also kept her company and occupied her time. She had a beautiful golden retriever, and she spent quite a bit of money at the groomers to keep him looking like a show dog. Cindy often worried about him, especially since he was now a senior dog. Sadly, he had a few expensive trips to the vet lately.

As much comfort as her dog brought her, Cindy was too sick to walk him around the neighborhood anymore. Jim took over the dog walking duties and Cindy spent the afternoons in bed with her computer on her lap online shopping. It had become one of her favorite hobbies.

Right before she had gotten sick, they had bought a new condo in Seattle. The new place sat empty and it was a blank canvas that she could decorate from her bed. Cindy ordered all kinds of furnishings and decorations online. Boxes upon boxes arrived at the Seattle condo and her family and friends had to stop by on a weekly basis to put the packages away.

Cindy was halfway through her treatment and we were both excited because Serena's parents were coming to Maui to visit her. Serena had invited us to dinner to meet them.

Unfortunately, Cindy was not feeling well and would not be able to join us. She was disappointed that she wasn't going to meet Serena's parents. I assured her she would meet them eventually since they lived in Washington and Serena would be in our lives forever. I told Cindy I would call her in the morning and tell her everything about Serena's parents.

We met for dinner at a local pizza joint. Serena's parents flew in from Seattle the night before and they were jet lagged, but they both had the same cheery personalities as Serena.

Her mother was lovely and vibrant like Serena: she wore a colorful flower-print dress and beautiful feathered earrings. Her father wore a bright purple golf shirt and they gave off a positive radiant light just like their daughter. Serena introduced them to us, "Roland and Sarah, these are my parents."

Roland shook their hands and in Swiss German said, "Gruezi."

Her mother said, "Serena has told us all about you two. Sarah you are so brave. And how incredible that Roland is from Switzerland. Thank you for taking care of Serena and being her friends."

We sat down at a table and ordered pizzas. Roland was chatting away in Swiss German to Serena's parents and I asked Serena what she was planning on doing while her parents were visiting. They were going to go hiking, snorkeling, and take a sunset whale-watching cruise.

The night was wrapping up and Serena's father said, "You and Roland must come visit us in Washington. It's beautiful with the mountains, it's similar to Switzerland."

"I know we should. My friend, Cindy has a condo there and one day we will all have to meet there! It would be a lot of fun."

I thanked them for having such a caring and loving daughter. It was a blessing to have Serena as my nurse, and it was truly special having her as my friend.

In the morning, I called Cindy and told her all about the dinner. "Cindy, Serena's parents are so kind and sweet. You would love them. We talked about meeting them in Seattle sometime. Now we have to visit you when you're there and all get together!"

Cindy laughed, "That sounds delightful! And Washington just legalized marijuana!"

chapter 23

SEA TURTLES

After her parents flew back to Seattle, Serena had texted me about getting together. We planned a double date night with her and Dan. Serena loved going through the newspaper to find new and different upcoming events to attend. She had read about a painting class where you could drink wine and paint. None of us had been there before and it sounded fun. We picked a weekend night and decided to go.

Roland and I arrived at the art party store and walked through the open door. Serena and Dan were already there and greeted us when we walked in. The painting instructor was setting up her things on a small stage in the front of the room. Against the wall, was a small table with plastic cups, napkins, beer and wine for us to partake in. Serena and I filled up our cups with red wine, and the boys drank beer. She held up her cup and said, "Thanks for joining us tonight. This is going to be so much flippin fun!"

I raised my cup and laughed. Serena never swore; instead, she substituted dirty words with different words and phrases. She would say things like "oh sugar" or "honey buckets." It was a charming character trait that I loved about her.

The boys were chatting together and looking around the room, when Serena said to me, "I love the two of you. Dan and I have only been going out a few months, and you guys have been together for years. How do you keep the magic alive?"

I shrugged my shoulders and said, "I guess it's knowing that we love and respect each other. It's not just the ups and downs that make us stronger but also an inner peace that we will be there for each other no matter what."

"That's so wonderful to hear, you really found your soul mate when you met Roland."

The instructor announced that it was time to take our seats. There were a few long tables set up in the room, with easels and blank canvases sitting on them. Paintbrushes and paper plates were arranged at each seat and the instructor told us to fill the plates with different colors of acrylic paint.

We all looked at the stage and watched the instructor as she guided us how to paint the subject. That evening, we were to paint a sea turtle. I looked down at my ring finger and admired my turtle tattoo. Roland was next to me and carefully dipped his paintbrush in the navy-blue paint. He started on the background and then stepped back from his canvas. I could see he was thinking and planning on what he was going to paint next.

Roland was meticulous and pensive, where I was rushed and impatient. When we worked together it usually entailed me creating a mess and Roland cleaning it up and fixing it. I once brought a computer desk home that had to be assembled. I ripped the box open and had all of the pieces strewn across the floor. I tossed the directions aside and looked at the picture on the box. A few hours later with half of the pieces still lying on the floor, I looked at the picture on the box and said, "Good enough."

Roland had to take the desk apart and read the instructions thoroughly before even picking up a piece. It irritated me; I just wanted it to be done. I watched him read the instructions and said hurry up. I looked at our paintings and our differences clearly showed up on the canvas.

My sea turtle was rough edged and messy looking. Roland had always been a perfectionist and his piece of art was impressive. He ended up giving his painting to one of his clients as a gift, and it still hangs on their condo wall. My painting wound up on the floor in our home office.

Roland was the yin to my yang and Serena was right, I found my soul mate.

⁓⁓

After many discussions, Grace followed through with her plans to get me into stand-up paddling. She planned a session to teach me the basics. I was excited but anxious and my stomach was filled with butterflies. Grace was already there when I got to the beach. She was waiting for me with her bathing suit on and her blond hair was tied back in a ponytail.

The boards and paddles were lying on the sand and I strapped the surf leash around my ankle. I was shaking a little and Grace put her hand on my arm and assured me. "Sarah, everything is okay. You're going to be okay, and I'm going to be paddling right beside you."

The winter swells had arrived and there was large surf, so we decided to stay close to shore. I put the board in the water and climbed on slowly. It was large and stable, and I sat on my knees and slowly paddled around in the shallow water. Grace directed me to look straight at the horizon when I tried to stand up. She said, "Get some momentum and then try to stand up. The board will balance better when it's moving."

I looked over at her and wobbled off the board and fell in the water. She paddled over to me and I pulled myself back on the board. "Sarah, take your time. We don't have to be anywhere or do anything. Relax and have fun."

After a few failed attempts, I was able to stand up on the board. The wind was in my hair and the sun was shining. I looked straight ahead, and it looked like there were diamonds shimmering on the ocean's surface. I was smiling and I thought to myself, *I did it!*

chapter 24

MELE KALIKIMAKA

indy was inching closer and closer to being done with her chemotherapy. Unfortunately, her white blood cell count was low again during December, delaying her final chemo session. During one of our regular morning calls, she had a complete meltdown and was screaming on the phone with me. Cindy was supposed to be done with chemo before Christmas, but now she wouldn't be. I tried to calm her down and said, "Cindy, there is nothing you can do about it."

"I'm so mad! I want to have the best Christmas party, and I don't want to be too tired to have it."

"Have the party on the week your off chemo. Try to take it easy during the day and Jim, will help you set up everything for the party."

"I could scream, I'm so annoyed, but you're right. I guess I can do that. I just want it to be perfect."

"Cindy, it will be perfect, no matter what happens."

I was excited about the holiday season and the radio stations played Christmas music all day long to celebrate the time of year. Roland and I were invited to several Christmas parties and our calendar was full almost every night of the week. It was difficult to stay on Dora's diet and I gave myself some leeway when it came to my eating and drinking.

We were getting ready to take Roland's employees out for a Christmas dinner when Roland sat down and said, "I want to talk to you about how much you've been eating and drinking."

I got defensive. "Roland it's the holidays, and I'm enjoying myself."

"Do you have to eat crap and drink alcohol to enjoy yourself?"

"Why are you bringing this up now?"

"Because I'm disappointed in you. You're not taking care of yourself; you are supposed to be eating healthy and not drinking beer all night long."

I was irritated and said, "Whatever Roland, I'm trying to have fun."

He was frustrated. "The way we eat is supposed to be a life plan. It's not going to be something you do off and on. Do you want to get sick again?"

I started to see red and lost my temper. I yelled at him, "I can't live like this anymore!"

The only thing Roland and I argued about during my treatment was food. He was strict with what we ate, and I knew it was because he was afraid of losing me. His fear manifested into controlling my diet and it was driving me crazy.

I was generally fine with our diet, but I thought it was okay to occasionally have fun and pig out on foods we weren't supposed to eat. There was no compromise with Roland, and he continued on with his rant about my eating and drinking. He yelled back at me. "Do you want to get cancer again? I can't lose you!"

"Why are you doing this?" I screamed. "We are having the best time with our friends, and you have to ruin it. Why go out and have fun, if I can't do anything? Why do you have to ruin our happiness?"

I was so upset that I grabbed the first thing I laid my eyes on, my ugly sea turtle painting, and hurled it across the room with all the might of my fury. The ocean background left a blue mark from the paint on the blank wall. My anger spent; I sank to my knees crying. Roland approached and tentatively reached out to me. We sat on the floor together and both cried. "Roland, I don't want to live in fear anymore and I don't want you to either."

The next morning, he made my green smoothie as usual and didn't say a word about my diet and I drank every drop of it.

It was time for Cindy's Christmas party. She had plenty of energy and was busy finishing up last minute details. She followed my advice and rested during the week. Everyone invited was asked to bring a dish to share, so Cindy wouldn't have to spend the whole day cooking. She usually made beef Wellington for Christmas dinner, but she knew Roland and I didn't eat meat anymore, so she served king crab legs as the main course instead.

When we arrived at her house, we saw that Cindy had gone all out: the long dining room table was spread with all the Christmas china, formal place cards, fancy napkin holders, and miniature porcelain Christmas trees filled with chocolates were at every seat.

Cindy's friends were arriving, and everyone was full of holiday spirit. Serena and Dan were invited, and Cindy welcomed them at the door with glasses of champagne. She was indeed, well-rested and was running around with her Santa hat on, getting everything in order. I stood in awe of Cindy. Watching her interact with all the guests and how she made everyone feel special, it was her true Christmas gift to everyone.

We all sat down to eat and there were party favors on everyone's plates. Cindy told us they were Christmas crackers and instructed us all to break them open. Ribbons and glitter spilled out of them along with a cheerful holiday message.

Cindy was having a blast and she made a toast to everyone. We held up our glasses and by the end of the night, we were all "three sheets to the wind," as Cindy would say.

chapter 25

ONLY THE GOOD DIE YOUNG

I went to visit Cindy on her final day of chemotherapy, and she was ready to get back to her normal life. When I entered the room, she looked up from her phone. "Sarah, I just bought tickets to Seattle for the summer."

I could see how excited she was, but I was alarmed that she bought the tickets so quickly. "That's great Cindy, but don't you think you should have waited to see how you feel after your radiation treatments?"

Her eyes grew big, "Wait! I've been waiting for over a year now. I haven't left the island for a year, and Jim and I are going."

I saw that I upset her and quickly changed the subject. I took a flower lei out of my bag and put it over her head and said, "It's almost time for us to burn our bags!"

~ 113 ~

"Yes, I can't wait to burn this stupid thing. Two months of radiation and I will finally be done with all of this."

Cindy started her radiation treatments the day after her 60th birthday. She didn't have a birthday party and wasn't thrilled about turning sixty. She hated the idea of being seen as old. I tried to cheer her up and remind her that she was lucky to be alive.

I told her about a lovely post on Emalia's memorial Facebook page that mentioned how Emalia would use the words "make" or "made" when referring to someone's birthday, instead of "turn" or "turning." Emalia believed that getting older was an achievement, not something to be ashamed of. Cindy listened, and I joked that she still had the energy and attitude of a twenty-year-old.

I offered to take her to the cancer center for her radiation treatments, but Cindy refused. She wanted to drive herself. Radiation was unknown territory for me, so she explained the process to me over the phone. "They mark an area on my stomach, and a machine radiates that spot for a few seconds and that's it," Cindy said.

It sounded simple enough, but I knew it was not good. I thought about my neighbor Anne and the horrible side effects that she had to endure the rest of her life from the radiation. I was relieved that I didn't have to have it but now I was worried about Cindy.

Almost immediately, the radiation made Cindy sick and she barely left the house. I could hear that she was in pain from the way she spoke, and it made me nervous. I wanted her treatments to be over just as much as she did.

— — ﹏ ﹍ ﹍

I was at the local market buying vegetables one day, and ran into Anne's friend, Tammy Lynn. She was wearing bright pink glasses and had her usual plastic neon flower in her hair. "Bill is back," she said.

"Oh, that's great news. I can't wait to see them. I tried to call Anne this fall and never heard back," I said.

Tammy Lynn gave me an alarming look and said, "You don't know?"

I must have looked perplexed. "Anne is dead," she said.

"What?"

"They went to the mainland for the summer and Anne was diagnosed with cancer. She passed away in December."

It was a surreal moment getting the news standing in the middle of the market. I was trying to process what I had been told and my face went numb. I awkwardly thanked her for letting me know and hurried home.

I put my vegetables away and walked up the street in a rush. I knocked on the door of Bill and Anne's house, and an unfamiliar woman answered the door. I learned she was a family friend and the tears had already started to form in my eyes. I looked at her and said, "I am a neighbor of Anne's and I just heard the news."

The woman let me in, and Bill got up from the sofa to hug me, as I began to cry. I gathered myself and sat down, as Bill told me the whole story. Before they left for their trip to the mainland, Anne was diagnosed with cervical cancer. "It was a small surgery, and everything was supposed to be okay after that. But they completely missed another tumor. It was stage four," Bill said.

Bill and Anne decided to stay on the mainland for her treatment, so she passed away there. I was physically shaking at the news. Questions raced through my mind: *How? What? Why?* Instead, I asked about Buddy the dog. Anne's friend who answered the door informed me that some family friends took him in.

Bill was going to be on the island for the next month to get things settled, and his daughters were flying out in a week to help him. I told him to call me if he needed anything and I walked home, drained and feeling empty inside. I was out of tears and filled with sadness for a woman I knew briefly, and the hope of a future friendship extinguished.

Bill and his daughters invited Roland and I over for dinner one evening. The younger daughter, Leigh, was a new mother with a baby girl. I couldn't help but notice how much she looked like a young Anne, with the same petite stature and feisty grin as her mother. The older daughter Laura was newly married, and she showed me photos of the wedding and it looked like a gorgeous affair. It was bittersweet to flip through the photos and see pictures of Bill and Anne holding each other, celebrating the marriage of their daughter.

It was a sad time for all of them. At one point Laura started talking about Anne and said, "Being at this house without my mom..." but she couldn't continue the thought and burst into tears.

It was depressing, having a newly remodeled house, and all their plans for the future had disappeared in an instant. Sitting in the renovated house I thought, never in a million years did anyone expect Anne to be gone.

I asked myself, *how did the doctors miss it? How in a matter of months was Anne dead?* I was in disbelief and I remembered what Anne said to me before she left for the mainland. "I'm living proof that only the good die young."

I was upset and the feelings of anger arose. Life was so unfair and cruel. I thought to myself, *Why did Anne and Emalia have to die? Why was everyone dying of cancer? Why was this happening? I'm not supposed to die. I'm too young to die. I don't want to die.* Their fate was a dark reminder of Cindy's and my own cancer.

The girls were staying a few weeks on Maui and planned to clean out the closets in the house while Bill tried to figure out his next steps. I told them I would stop by often and we exchanged phone numbers. Roland and I hugged Bill goodbye and we walked back home in the dark in silence.

Grace followed through with her plans to get me into stand-up paddling and set up another lesson. I was struggling with my anxiety after learning about Anne, and I insisted Roland come with me. He was slightly annoyed and stressed out from work and he pleaded over the phone, "Do I really have to come? Grace is there and you have been fine going in the water."

"No, you have to come." I said, and hung up the phone.

I remembered what Dora said about visualizing the positive and I decided to drive to the beach in the morning before my lesson with Grace to get motivated. I arrived at the beach and started thinking about everything that could go wrong and about all the bad things that happened to me. As my mind raced, every insecurity and fear came to the surface. I started to cry and shake, as the fears closed around me like a vice, or a panic attack. I had to get out of there.

Tears were falling down my face as I got in my car. I called Grace and said, "I can't go. I can't do this anymore."

Grace was confused by my reaction and tried to reassure me. "Everything is okay. Let's just meet at the beach this afternoon and see how you feel when you get there."

I felt childish and with my chin shaking, said, "Okay."

When I got home, I was in bed waiting for Roland to come home. He found me lying under the sheets with tears in my eyes. "Are you really that afraid of the ocean?" he asked. "I thought you felt better."

I wiped the tears from my cheeks and said, "I don't know who I am anymore. I don't know what I'm supposed to do. I don't want to be lost anymore."

I sat up in bed and he hugged me and said, "Come on let's get ready, we're going to do this together."

My phone beeped and I saw it was a text from Laura. Her sister had left a few days before and she wanted to hangout before she flew back home. I text her back and wrote that I was going to the beach to stand up paddle. She wrote back, "What time are you going? My dad and I would like to join you."

I was filled with confidence and texted her back the time, I thought, *I'm not alone, it's going to be fine, I've got Roland and my friends with me.*

We got to the beach and Grace was there waiting with enough boards for all of us. Grace led the way and Bill paddled on his knees. Laura was a pro, standing tall on the board and I paddled next to Roland. As we made our way down the coastline, Laura pointed out to something in the water. My heart dropped and I thought the worst, was it a shark?

Laura yelled out, "Look, it's a baby manta ray. The water is so clear you can see it lying on the sand."

I paddled toward her and saw the little dark shape of the ray. Nothing bad happened out in the water and when we finished putting the boards on the beach, I thought about Emalia and Anne. I remembered the story about Emalia and the Aumakuas. Emalia had come back as an owl and I knew it was silly to think that Anne showed up as a manta ray, but I was comforted by the thought that she was watching over us on the water that day.

chapter 26

BURN BABY BURN

Cindy's two months of radiation were over, and her doctor scheduled a CT/PET scan to check for cancer. She had her follow-up appointment to find out the results of the scan and I called her when she got home from the cancer clinic. "Hey Cindy, how did everything go?"

"Hey kiddo, I'm tired today. Can we talk later?"

I ignored what she said and was impatient. "Well? What were the results?" I asked.

"The scan showed all clear."

"Oh my gosh, Cindy that is terrific! Did the doctor say anything else?"

"Sarah, I'm exhausted. I will call you later okay?"

"Sounds good! I will call you tomorrow morning," and before I hung up the phone I said, "This is the best

~ 121 ~

news Cindy. I hope you get some rest and get ready, because we have a party to plan!" I hung up the phone relieved that she was cancer free.

Cindy and I got busy planning our bag-burning party. I was excited and couldn't stop smiling at the thought of setting our chemo bags on fire. We decided to have a potluck on the beach. Cindy made a list with the guest's names and what they would bring. I was going to bring wood for the fire.

We had our party on the unofficially dubbed Valentine's Beach, so named because Cindy and Jim went there once on Valentine's Day. It was a secluded beach and difficult to get to. To drive down to the beach you needed a four-wheel drive vehicle, or you would have to park next to the side of the road and walk down a steep dirt path.

All of Cindy's friends were there and Julie and Grace came. Serena and Dan were among the last to arrive and I ran up to them. "Wow, you made it! Did you have trouble finding the beach?"

Serena had her beach chair in her hand, "This spot is hidden girl. We drove past it twice before seeing your car parked in the grass."

"I'm so happy you're here. I can't wait to toss my bag in the fire!"

Serena reached into her bag and took out a sparkling plastic necklace from the dollar store and a plastic pink tiara. "I got you and Cindy these to celebrate the occasion.

I laughed, "Serena, these are awesome! Thank you so much."

"I had to get the best for my two favorite patients. Now, last chance, are you sure you don't want to keep your bags? I have a bedazzler machine at home and we can bedazzle them up!"

"Tempting as it sounds, I'm still going to throw my bag in the fire and then it will be gone forever."

Cindy and I put on our tiaras and necklaces and we were the queens for the night. Everyone ate, drank and talked as the sun set over the ocean. Jim formed a circle with some rocks and dropped the firewood in the middle of it. The fire crackled and we watched the sky turn pink then red, then black. Everyone was sitting around the fire on their beach chairs and I asked Cindy if she was ready. "I was born ready," she answered.

I grabbed Roland's hand and stood up. Cindy, Jim, Roland and I held each other by the waist, and everyone started clapping. Serena started chanting, "Burn them, burn them, burn them."

I looked over at Cindy and said, "You first."

"I have a better idea. Let's throw them in at the same time."

We smiled at each other and there was a silent look we gave each other. We had been through so much in the last year together and we knew how special this moment was. We lifted our arms in the air and tossed our bags into the fire. Everyone started cheering and I watched the bag catch on fire and it slowly disappeared into the flames. The cancer was behind us now and it was finally over.

chapter 27

MEET THE PARENTS

My parents came out to visit in April. They had not been to Maui in thirteen years. My mother was terrified of flying, so it was a big deal that they were coming. She went to the doctor prior to the trip, and they prescribed her some medicine so she could be relaxed for the nine-hour flight to Maui. I was excited to see my parents and couldn't wait for them to meet all of my friends.

When I moved away from Ohio, I had started the routine of calling my parents every Sunday morning to keep in touch. We had a healthy relationship and throughout my treatment, my mom sent hopeful, cheery cards to me. I loved my parents, but I hadn't spent a lot of time with them in recent years.

When my mom got off the plane, she grabbed my face and looked me straight in the eyes and we both smiled. She saw that her daughter was healthy and well. I hugged my dad and it was a relief for them to see that their little girl was okay.

I took my mother's hand and asked, "How did you do on the flight?"

"I did ok, but your father's hand is sore from me squeezing it so hard when we landed. It was so windy, the plane bounced up and down."

We picked up their luggage at the baggage claim and walked to my car. "Well Roland is at work so you won't see him until later, but you will get to meet Doodle. Who is watching Sophie while you're here?" I said.

My mom opened the car door and sat down in the back seat. "Oh, your brother is watching her."

Sophie was the newest family member; she was a little twenty-pound bichon shih tzu mix. My mom researched the breed and wanted a cuddly lap dog when she picked Sophie out of the litter. To my mother's dismay, Sophie wanted to be outside, chasing the squirrels and digging in the dirt, instead of cuddling on the couch next to her. She joked that Sophie turned out to be like me, a free independent spirit that wouldn't listen to her.

All of my friends were eager to meet my parents, and everyone claimed some time to visit while they were staying with us. Julie and Grace stopped by the house and I introduced them to my parents. We had dinner with Serena, and my mother loved that Serena dressed in such flair, color and style. My father thanked her for taking such good care of me when I went through my chemotherapy.

Cindy made a point of inviting my parents over for lunch and said, "I want your parents to know that you have people that love you and will take care of you here."

We arrived at Cindy's house and she greeted us at the front door, and she had her dining room table all set with the dishes and silverware out. Cindy knew a great deal about my parents through our countless discussions.

I had warned her in advance that my parents were kind of square. They never swore, and they didn't smoke or drink alcohol. So, there were no margaritas or gin and tonics served, only lemonade and iced tea.

Cindy was fascinated by the fact that my father was a retired FBI agent, and she couldn't help but ask him all sorts of questions about his career. We all had a laugh, joking that when Roland first met him, my dad was seriously considering hooking him up to a lie detector test, ready to interrogate and terrify his new son-in-law.

My father was a good man and he had a quiet and stoic character. Being the only daughter, my dad had a soft spot for me and let me get away with certain things that the boys would get in trouble for. I was his little princess even though I was a tomboy.

I sat at the table and was happy that my mom finally got to meet Cindy. She knew about her from phone conversations, but I never talked in depth about our relationship and the bond that we had, having the same cancer diagnosis. Cindy and I were like two schoolgirls, chatting away at lunch and my mom laughed and commented on our non-stop banter. "Can any of us get a word in between the two of you?!" She asked.

Cindy turned to my mother and started to ask her questions about her life and then she asked my mom how she came about adopting me. My mom answered, "Well, we had three healthy young boys and the church we went to at the time worked with an agency that helped families adopt Korean children. I knew there were so many orphaned babies in the world that needed love and I always wanted a girl."

"That is a beautiful story," Cindy said.

My mom continued, "The orphanage in Korea gave her the name of Jung Hwa and they told us it means calm flower.

"That is too precious, thank you for sharing that. Now, before I forget, I want to take a picture of you guys," Cindy said, as she got up from the table.

She came back with her camera and held it up to her face. I put my arm around my mom and dad and when I started to smile Cindy said, "Sarah, don't do that with your eyes."

"What? I'm not doing anything."

"You always open your eyes wide when you get your picture taken."

My mom laughed and said, "You know, when Sarah was five years old, she became a U.S. citizen. We had a private ceremony for her to be naturalized with a judge. When the judge finished, she asked him if her eyes were round now that she was an American."

We all laughed at the story and I thought about all of my childhood insecurities and remembered that I was always proud of being adopted. I looked over at my mom and was thankful for all the love and strength that she had bestowed on me.

chapter 28

I MADE IT

I was amazed how the time flew by and a whole year had passed since my first chemo treatment. During my chemo, I told myself I was going to be stronger, not just physically, but emotionally and spiritually. Finally acknowledging that I let fear control my life, a huge weight had been lifted off my shoulders. I wanted to surf and enjoy the ocean again. Even with the neuropathy in my feet, nothing was going to stop me from my goal.

Roland and I bought new stand-up paddleboards, and I started making paddle dates with Julie and Grace. I fell in love with stand-up paddling and being out on the water. I would gaze down into the ocean and look at the reef. It was beautiful to see the yellow, pink and purple coral heads. Colorful tropical fish swam below my board and sea turtles glided next to me as they surfaced for air.

Cindy knew about my new interest in stand-up paddling and she told me that she had a friend that also stand-up paddled. Her friend was interested in doing a community bonding non-competitive, water event exclusively for women.

It was a down-winder, which was a stand-up paddle along the coastline. You would begin on one end of the beach, and the wind and current would push you, miles down the coast. You ended up at a different beach, far away from where you began, and you needed to shuttle vehicles around to get your equipment and gear back to your car.

Grace had been trying to talk me into going with her on a down-winder and I had always been too scared, though the thought of going out with hundreds of women in an organized event appealed to me and seemed safe. Grace and some friends already signed up for the event and I joined them.

On the morning of the event, I had arrived at the beach and the organizers were gathering all of the participants to join in a circle to stretch and do yoga to warm our muscles up. There were at least a hundred women there and it was a sight to see all of the colorful paddleboards lying on the sand.

The founder of the event came out with a microphone and talked about how she started the movement to inspire women everywhere to be active in the community. She wanted to give women more confidence in the water and in life and we listened in awe. It was a beautiful message and we were all there for that purpose.

For the event, the conditions were perfect. The wind was light, and the ocean was calm and flat as a lake. Being on the water with all of these women was exhilarating and there was a wonderful camaraderie between everyone. I paddled with confidence and ease. People were on the beach cheering for everyone and when we finished there was music playing and people were dancing on the sand. I sent Cindy pictures of the event and she thought she would sign up and participate next year.

It was already May and my birthday was coming up. My friend, Julie, called me to see if I wanted to surf and hangout. I was up for it and she came and picked me up at my house. When she arrived, she was grinning from ear to ear and said, "Hey, before we go surfing, I have to drop something off at the post office."

"No problem," I said, but was wondering why she was overly excited.

We drove to the post office parking lot and she said, "Oh, I forgot I have to get something across the street. Get out of the car and come with me."

"I don't mind waiting in the car."

"No, I need you to come with me," she said.

I looked at her with trepidation, "Really?"

She was grabbing my arm, "Come on, it will only be a minute."

I got out of the car and followed her into a hair salon. She couldn't contain herself any longer and said, "Surprise! I scheduled a haircut for you. I knew you would never get your haircut, but you need to do something to it before your birthday party."

My hair was still thin, but new curly hair was growing in. I had a strange mullet of thin, straight hair in the back and thick new curls coming out shorter. I knew it looked odd, but I always wore a hat and didn't think much of it. A lot of my girlfriends joked that they secretly wanted to have me do a complete makeover, like the ones they did on television. Julie had tricked me, and I got my first real haircut in over a year.

My hair was cut short and it was stylish with the curls. I sat in the salon chair and looked over at Julie. She was quite pleased with herself and took a picture of my new do on her phone. I laughed and thought about how Julie always made me laugh or smile. She was like an audience cheering and laughing and everyone was a stand-up comedian. I had never met anyone that laughed as much as Julie.

The hairdresser took my apron off and brushed off a few strands of hair on my shoulder. I stood up and hugged Julie and said, "Well, thanks for the birthday gift. Roland will be happy I got a haircut. Now, let's get ready for my party."

I thought about Emalia and I had made it to age thirty-nine. It was my accomplishment and I felt lucky to be alive. I ended up throwing a birthday party at my house, with about fifty guests, I wanted to celebrate life with all of the people I loved. Cindy and Jim arrived, and they brought their "punch" full of tequila like a couple of college kids, and Cindy was giggling like crazy. I wondered how much pot she had smoked beforehand. I remembered the last birthday and that Cindy was in the hospital and what we had been through in a year. I hugged Cindy and said, "Here you are! You made it to my party this year!"

We put our drinks together and toasted. Cindy gave off an infectious laugh and said, "Here's to many more birthdays and parties!"

All of my friends were there, and I was on cloud nine. I grabbed Roland and we ran into the bedroom. Julie, being the party queen, had given us ridiculous sumo wrestling outfits to wear and we put them on. The costumes were stuffed full and weighed a ton. It felt like wearing a beanbag. We waddled outside the room and everyone burst into laughter. Outside on the grass, we wrestled each other, to everyone's amusement. Roland knocked me over and I was like a turtle on its shell. It was hysterical and we took off the suits and all of the guests tried them on afterwards. Laughter filled the air.

Julie came out with my birthday cake and the candles were all lit up. The numbered candles were on backwards, and I blew out the "93" with a full heart. And like the past year, I didn't wish for a thing because being alive was enough of a gift.

Right after my birthday, my port was finally taken out. I also had my now-yearly tests: a colonoscopy and CAT scan. After the tests were taken, I was confident I would be given a clean bill of health, but Roland was anxious every time. I tried to stay positive and when the results came back all clear with no signs of cancer, I called Roland and we celebrated.

chapter 29

MAINLAND CALLING

As summer approached, Cindy and Jim were busy getting ready to head to the mainland. It was going to be a summer of visiting old friends and family. They were finally going to get to stay in their new condo in Seattle. Cindy was ready to get her life back in full swing after it had been put on hold for a year and a half.

Cindy was completely over everything and anything that had to do with cancer. The doctors recommended that she keep her port in after her radiation treatments, but she wanted it removed as soon as possible. I had my port in for a year and it wasn't so bad, and I said, "Cindy they have you keep the port, in case the cancer comes back."

"Sarah, if the cancer came back, I would not do another treatment. I'm never going through that again, I'm done."

~ 136 ~

"Okay," I said, and there was no point of trying to convince her otherwise, because she had made up her mind and her port was taken out.

While Cindy was planning her trip, she tried to figure out what to do with her beloved dog. He had bitten a man on the street once and even though he was older and less aggressive, she still had to watch him like a hawk, when strangers were around.

When Jim and Cindy went on a river cruise three years earlier, they had to board the dog in a kennel. To Cindy's horror, he came back sick and with blood coming out of his eyes and she promised him that she would never have him kenneled again. Now that they were leaving for three months the dog issue came up.

I came up with a great solution. My matchmaking skills had officially been proven, as Serena and Dan were planning on moving in together and were looking for a new place to live. "Cindy, why don't you have Serena and Dan watch the dog when you are gone? It will be perfect. You would give them three months to find a place to live and they can watch your baby," I said.

"I love Serena. Do you think she would mind?"

"Well, you could at least ask. I mean, she took care of us, didn't she?"

Cindy laughed and said, "That's true, and the dog doesn't talk back."

Serena thought it was a great idea and wanted to help Cindy too. It took a lot of stress off Cindy, knowing she had loving people taking care of her dog and that he wouldn't have the emotional turmoil of going somewhere strange for months on end. It was agreed upon that Serena and Dan would dog and house sit over the summer.

Sadly, Cindy's dog died right before they left to the mainland. Cindy was devastated, upset, and heartbroken. Her wonderful companion was gone.

Cindy was sad and depressed but stayed active with a list of things she needed to do before they left. Serena and Dan had already given notice to their landlords, so Cindy and Jim allowed them to stay at their house for the summer.

Cindy was busy getting everything in order in the house, deciding what to pack away and what to leave out for Serena. She made room in her closet and Jim showed Dan how to use the lawn mower and all the other appliances around the house. Cindy insisted on hiring an army of housekeepers to come up and clean the house from top to bottom.

"Cindy, you're leaving, and Serena doesn't care how clean the house is," I said.

"I know, but I need to have everything perfect for them," Cindy said.

The night before Jim and Cindy flew out for the summer, we drove over to their house for dinner. In classic Cindy fashion, we were greeted with champagne at the door and a cheery, "Hey kiddo!"

She handed us our glasses and we all toasted. Cindy started telling us, their itinerary for the summer. A full road trip up and around the West Coast was planned, where they would visit family and friends almost every day. Then, they were going to drive back to Seattle and were planning on having houseguests throughout the summer. It was a full and hectic schedule and Cindy was making up for the lost time.

I drank my champagne too quickly and dropped my glass, "Oh shit!" I said.

There was glass all over the hardwood floor and I knew Cindy was going to be mad. The champagne was in nice, expensive crystal glasses. Nothing in their house was cheap. To my surprise, she laughed and helped me clean it all up. "These glasses were given to us as a wedding gift" she said.

Gee, thanks for making me feel better, I thought, but she continued, "They're just things. They can be bought and replaced, don't worry about it."

It was nice to witness a change in Cindy, there was a softness to her, being close to death changed her. I was sad Cindy was leaving but happy for her too. The trip gave her something to be excited for. We had dinner and promised to stop by the house and see how Serena was doing. Cindy said, "Now, don't think you can sleep in while I'm gone. I'm still going to call you at 6:30, It is only a three-hour time difference on the West Coast.

I smiled and said, "I wasn't planning on sleeping in at all. And you better answer when I call."

After dinner, we all hugged goodbye and when I walked out the door, I said, "See you guys in three months."

The next morning, they hopped on a plane. They were busy meeting all their friends and family, but it didn't affect our phone calls. The calls kept coming and if I was ever busy or called later in the morning, Cindy greeted me with a, "Hey kiddo, what happened to you? What did you do, sleep in?"

It's something special to look forward to hearing your friends voice every day.

On one of our morning calls from the mainland, Cindy said, "I'm going to tell you something, but you have to promise not to freak out."

I rolled my eyes even though I knew she couldn't see me over the phone, and said, "Okay, I won't freak out. What am I not supposed to freak out about?"

"Well, I had some blood in my stool," she whispered.

A part of me did freak out, but I didn't want to make her worry and said, "I mean, we did have colon cancer; do you think it could be from a hemorrhoid?"

"Maybe, I have been a little constipated lately," she said.

I thought for a moment, I tried to stay calm and said, "Maybe it's from the radiation? Did you call the doctor?"

"I'm sure it's just a side effect from the radiation? That's probably it," she said with a sigh of relief in her voice.

I could hear from her tone that she already wanted to change the subject and I said, "Cindy, I think you should go to the doctor and have it checked out."

"Don't be silly, I'm going to wait to go to the doctor. Anyways, don't worry about it. I just wanted to see what you thought about it. Jim and I are having the best time out here. We just saw some old work buddies and now we are heading north, to see more friends."

"Well, if it happens again, you should go to the doctor," I said, trying to get her to refocus and I Googled the symptoms of radiation, as soon as we hung up. The list of side effects and complications were long. I was concerned but Cindy assured me she was fine and we both told ourselves it was nothing to be worried about.

chapter 30

SUMMER OF FUN

It became the summer of fun for me. I was in the water all the time. Grace had a stand-up surfboard. It was different than the other stand-up paddleboards we had because it was shaped and made specifically for catching waves.

After watching Grace surfing with her board, I quickly went out and bought one too. It felt great to be surfing again; it had been years since I caught a wave. Riding a wave, felt like dancing on the water. The power of the breaking wave picked up the surfboard and pushed the board forward. It was an adrenaline rush as I balanced so I wouldn't fall off the board. Once the ride was over, I wanted to catch another one, like a little kid at an amusement park. I still had to work on my balance, but I got better with every surf session.

I grew confident and all my fears about the water and sharks melted away. Dora was right: cancer woke me up, and I was now happier and healthier. I thought about Emalia and Anne a lot when I was out on the water. I was determined to live a full life for them. I faced my fears so I could do the things they couldn't. I was alive.

Julie and I went out for a surf session one afternoon. The waves were good, and sets were coming in consistently. Julie was like a teenager, which was amazing, since she was in her fifties. She loved surfing and was happy that I was out on the water with her. We had been out for three hours and my fingers looked like prunes from being in the water so long. "Julie, I'm exhausted, let's go in."

"I want to catch one more," she said.

Unfortunately, that "one more" meant at least three more waves. My legs were like logs on my board and I was too tired to even paddle. I looked behind me and saw a tiny wave coming in. It was not going to be a thrilling last wave, but I needed to catch it, to get back to shore.

I paddled for it and the minute the wave lifted the board up, I knew I was positioned wrong and wasn't going to catch the wave. The nose of my board went straight into the water and I tumbled past it and was tossed in the ocean. I surfaced and saw my board soaring vertical in the air. I looked up as the board came crashing down and hit me on the head. I saw stars for a brief moment, and I knew it was going to leave a bump.

I was able to crawl back onto my board and I felt like a tired wet dog. My hair was messy and all over the place. It covered my eyes and I moved it out of my face to see. I paddled to shore, panting with my tongue sticking out. Julie caught a wave in and started laughing. "What happened? You didn't catch a wave in?"

I was laughing too and said, "Did you see my board flying in the air? It hit me in the head."

"Oh boy, you are going to have a shiner for sure!"

Julie was right and the next morning I looked in the mirror and I had a big black eye. It was my first black eye ever, and I wore it like a badge of honor. I sent a picture of my black eye to Cindy, and when I called, she asked, "How's your shiner?"

She was in Seattle and was getting a manicure and pedicure when she answered the phone. "So, we met up with Serena's parents yesterday and they invited us over for dinner tonight. They are so lovely. I mean Serena's mother is gorgeous and wears the most divine perfume. Remind me to ask her what the name of it is, it's such a heavenly scent."

"It's so cool that you got to meet up with them. Roland and I are going up to your house tonight for dinner. Serena and Dan are going to grill some fish on the barbeque."

"Oh, tell Serena, thanks for letting me use her bicycle. There are some wonderful trails around the condo. Jim hikes and I ride along next to him on the bike."

"What a small world, huh? You're in Seattle with Serena's parents and we are going to your house with Serena."

"It is, isn't it? Well, Serena's father knows all the hikes and mountains around the area. Jim is going to pick his brain tonight and hopefully learn about some new trails to explore. They already invited us to go on a hike with them this weekend."

"Well, have a great dinner and tell them Roland and I say hello. I guess we have to come to Seattle next summer."

"Yes, our condo has a guest room with your name on it and we'll have the best time. You kids have fun tonight."

"You too. Talk to you tomorrow."

We arrived at Cindy's house and Serena greeted us at the door with a glass of wine. I joked and said, "Do you always greet your guests with wine at the door, or did you learn that from Cindy?"

"I learned it from the hostess with the mostest, Cindy," she said smiling. "Wow, look at your black eye. It didn't look that purple in the picture you sent me today."

"Isn't it cool? I've never had a black eye before."

We laughed, and I followed Serena through the house. Dan was out on the lanai grilling the fish. We stood outside enjoying the view. We could see the airplanes descending down the valley, heading towards the airport to land. There was a view of the harbor and we watched a cruise ship come into port. The sun was setting behind the mountains and we watched the houses sitting on the volcano, Haleakala, turn different shades of pink and orange from the setting sun.

After dinner, we played board games and Serena went into the bedroom and brought her phone out. She played a voicemail from her mother. "Hello Serena, we had Jim and Cindy over for dinner and had a wonderful evening. Hope you are having fun on Maui."

Serena and I were giggling like young girls at a slumber party listening to the voicemail. The idea of all of us being connected, miles away was awe-inspiring to us.

chapter 31

THE PADDLEBOARD

Cindy was having fun, but Jim was ready to come home. It had been a busy summer for them, and he was starting to miss Maui. They were coming back at the end of August, but that was a month and a half away.

One morning when I called Cindy, I could tell she was exhausted from all the guests they'd had at their condo over the summer. There was something wrong in her voice. In an agonized tone she said, "There was blood in my stool again. Lots of blood."

I was worried and knew she needed to get medical attention. I said, "Cindy, you have to go to the hospital!"

She moaned, "Ouch!"

"Cindy, please just go have it checked out," I pleaded.

"Ouch, my stomach hurts so much Sarah."

She moaned again in pain and softly said, "Okay, I think your right."

She yelled for Jim to come and I said, "Call me back when you have a chance and let me know you're okay."

I hung up the phone and felt panicked and helpless. I kept telling myself, "It's the side effects of the radiation, that's all."

The next day she called me from the hospital in Seattle. She had a CAT scan and they ran some tests but didn't find anything. "It's probably complications from the radiation. Or I must have eaten something that disagreed with me. I did have a tuna fish sandwich that smelled a little funny to me."

"So, they didn't find anything at all?"

"Nope, nothing. The hospital here is state of the art and modern and new."

"I'm glad you are getting top notch treatment. So, how are you feeling?" I asked.

"They gave me some painkillers and I feel fine. I'm almost positive it was something I ate. They are releasing me from the hospital in a few hours and I have so much to do when I get back to the condo."

I was worried but she reassured me that she was fine. Since I didn't have radiation, I couldn't compare symptoms, but I knew about the harmful lingering effects it could have on a body. I was relieved that nothing was wrong with Cindy.

A few days later, everything was back to normal and Cindy was telling me how much fun she was having. They were going on a road trip and planning on visiting some national parks for the week.

Roland and I were getting ready to leave on our own vacation, a river rafting trip down the Colorado River in the Grand Canyon. It was the kind of trip you checked off your bucket list and I had to reserve it a year in advance due to the limited availability. No phones, no cars, no TV, no computers, we were going to be completely unplugged and isolated from the rest of the world. It was a much-needed break for the both of us and I had wanted to do this trip years ago. There was always a reason to put the trip off, and I wasn't going to let that happen anymore. I told Cindy all about the trip and suggested that she and Jim do it next year.

A week before we were scheduled to leave for our trip, I got a strange text from Cindy: "I don't want your stand-up paddleboard anymore." I had been planning on selling my extra paddleboard to Serena, and told Cindy about it, but she insisted I sell her the board instead because she wanted one when she got back from the mainland.

In typical Cindy fashion, she had me send pictures of the board and I had to give her complete details about it. From the size, make and brand. Confused by the text, I called Cindy, but there was no answer. I called her again and she finally answered.

"Cindy, you made such a fuss about the board, and now you don't want it? I had to tell Serena she couldn't have the board, because you wanted it."

"Well, I changed my mind," she said.

"Fine, but what happened? Why did you suddenly change your mind?"

"I don't know. I just don't want it, and that's that," she said crossly. "I have to go; we are getting ready to leave."

Defeated, I said, "Okay, bye."

What is her problem? I wondered.

I called the next day as usual, but there was no answer. In fact, the whole week there was no answer. I asked myself, *"How can you talk to someone every day for years, and then suddenly just stop?"*

In the end, Serena, bought the paddleboard from me but I still hadn't heard anything from Cindy. The silence troubled me, and my feelings were hurt. When we got to the airport Roland squeezed my hand and said, "Stop thinking about Cindy, she is probably just really busy and stressed out. Knowing her, she is running around trying to do everything all at once. She always goes one hundred and ten percent and probably over did it and just needs some time to herself."

"I know, it's just that we have been through so much together."

"You guys will be fine. Give it some time and don't let this ruin our vacation."

"You're right. If she doesn't want to talk, that's her problem. I promise I won't let it bother me on our trip," I said as we boarded the plane.

Roland and I went on our rafting trip down the Colorado River, and it was awesome. There were twelve people on the tour, and we had a knowledgeable and friendly tour guide. We hiked to waterfalls, swam in turquoise blue pools, and enjoyed the colorful desert landscape. On the raft, we rode the rough rapids and the cold water hit us in the face. At night, we set up camp on remote beaches along the river. When I looked up the canyon walls at night, there were too many stars in the sky to count.

There was a nice family from the Seattle area also on the raft with us and we chatted all week long. I told them about Serena and Cindy and how we planned to go to Washington in the future now that we had friends there. I thought about Cindy a lot and knew she would love this trip too.

After our week on the river, we had to take a helicopter to get out of the canyon. We then boarded a small plane to Las Vegas. From the plane window, I saw the Vegas strip and we had definitely made it back to civilization. I turned on my cell phone for the first time in a week and a text popped up on the screen from Cindy: "You're probably having a blast on your trip. Call me when you get back."

I sat on our hotel bed, contemplating if I should call her immediately or make her wait in silence for a little while. I was still hurt that she didn't contact me and upset that I had to worry about her on my vacation. I waited a few hours and thought about it. One part of me said, *"I'm not going to call her back, and see how she likes being ignored.*

On the other hand, after everything I had learned over the last few years, I knew I had to let this go. I had to let go of my petty thoughts. Life was short, and I knew how Cindy could get when she got riled up about something. Plus, I missed talking to her.

Cindy answered the phone when I finally worked up the nerve to call her. "I don't feel so well, Sarah," she said. No cheerful, "Hey kiddo!" as I expected.

My stomach tightened and I said, "Cindy, go to the hospital now!"

"I think I need to," she said with some uncertainty.

"Yes, Cindy, go!" I urged.

"Okay, I will call you back." Then she hung up.

I sat there on the hotel bed in our room in Las Vegas trembling. I was so worried, and I asked myself, *What the hell is going on?*

I sighed, relieved that I had risen above my hurt feelings and called her. It was the last day of our vacation and I was on edge. The rest of the trip, I could not get Cindy out of my mind.

chapter 32

WE'RE ALL CONNECTED

When we got home from Las Vegas, Cindy was admitted to the hospital in Seattle. The doctors ran all different kinds of tests, but after a week they still couldn't figure out what was wrong. She didn't always answer her phone but would always call me back. I waited everyday with the hope that the doctors had finally found out what was wrong with her.

I woke up in the morning and my phone rang. It was Cindy. I frantically answered the phone, "Hey kiddo, sorry I wasn't feeling up to talking yesterday."

"It's okay Cindy. How are you doing? Did they find anything out yet?"

"I'm going into surgery this afternoon. They are going to do an exploratory surgery to see what's wrong."

~ 153 ~

My heart sank when she told me the news and I tried to sound positive. "Cindy, you're going to be alright."

I was filled with worry, and thought, *why is she so far away?* I tried to remain calm, "Do you want me to fly out and see you?"

I heard a tone of sadness in her voice when she said, "You would do that for me?"

"Of course, Cindy."

Her voice cracked, "I'm just an old woman."

My heart was breaking, "Cindy, you're more than that to me. You're..." I started to choke up and I couldn't get the words out.

"I know. I guess I am pretty special," she said softly.

My heart broke into pieces and the tears ran down my face. "I love you, Cindy."

"I love you, too."

I took a deep breath and tried to remain composed. "Okay, call me after the surgery."

When we hung up, all of my emotions came out and I opened the front screen door and started sobbing. I needed fresh air and I could feel the breeze lightly hit my face. I sat down with my phone in my hand and couldn't stop crying. *Why is she so far away? This pain and suffering is supposed to be over.*

I wiped the tears away and went back into the house. I sat down at the computer and started looking into flights to Seattle. I tried to think positive thoughts.

It's all symptoms from the radiation, I told myself over and over again.

When Cindy recovered from her surgery, she called me the next morning and had energy in her voice. She sounded strong, like the old Cindy.

"How are you feeling?" I asked.

"Are you sitting down?"

I was holding a cup of coffee, and Roland was talking to me about something. I shot him a look to shut up and I sat down on the couch.

"Sorry, Roland was asking me something, I'm sitting down now. What's going on?"

"Well, the cancer spread, and they've given me three to six months to live."

I had that feeling that I had experienced so often in the hospital. This was all a movie. It was not real. I couldn't even process her words, let alone figure out what to say, so a stupid, "How do you feel?" came out of my mouth.

"Sarah, I'm okay. I don't want you to go around feeling sorry for me, now. You promise not to do that?"

I was numb, "I promise."

My mind was racing, "Cindy, I'm going to fly out this afternoon and I can be there tomorrow."

"Sarah, don't do that. I don't want you to come."

I knew the feeling of being in the hospital and wanting to be left alone, "Ok, Cindy, I understand."

The rest of the conversation was a blur, and before I hung up, I said, "I love you Cindy."

"I love you, too."

I looked up at Roland and said, "They just gave Cindy three to six months to live."

He sat on the couch with his hand on his forehead. There were no tears, only silence. All during my treatment, I never thought I was going to die. I never thought Cindy was going to die. I always pushed those thoughts away. We were supposed to beat this together.

I got up from the couch and thought, *I can't cry in front of him. I have to be strong for Roland. I have to keep my shit together, even though my world is falling apart. Why is this happening?*

"I have to leave," I said.

Roland was still in shock and processing the news and he answered, "Okay."

I grabbed my car keys from the counter and got in the car and drove. The tears finally came out on the road and I was sobbing uncontrollably. It was worse than any nightmare because it was real. My world completely fell out from under me and I felt completely broken.

A few hours later when I was back home, my phone rang, and I saw that it was Dora calling. With everything that was going on with Cindy, I had forgotten that she had emailed me that she was coming to Maui this week. I answered the phone and she sounded tired and weak. "Hi, Sarah. I'm back on Maui. I got here two days ago and have been throwing up since. I'm really sick and I can't hold anything down."

"Dora, you should go to the doctor." *This is all too much.*

"I don't know Sarah," she said, clearly worried, "I haven't been this sick for years. I'm so weak. I can barely get out of my bed to use the bathroom. I'm all alone and I can't even drink water without throwing up."

"Dora, do you want me to come and get you and take you to the hospital?"

"Would you do that for me?" she asked faintly.

"Of course. I'm going to leave my house now and I will be at your place in twenty minutes."

"Oh, Sarah, thank you so much. I will try and get dressed."

I got in my car and headed towards Dora's condo. I was still reeling from Cindy's news in the morning but knew I had to be there for Dora. I called Roland to let him know what was going on and assured him that I would keep him posted. I arrived at Dora's condo and knocked on the door. Dora answered the door in her pajamas and looked pale and faint.

"Hi Sarah. Thanks for coming over. I was trying to look for something to wear. I'm just so tired."

"Dora, I think I should take you to the emergency room. You are probably really dehydrated."

"I hate the doctors; I haven't seen one in years. When I'm sick, I usually always get better on my own."

She lifted her finger up at me and held her mouth shut with her hand and grabbed a small plastic garbage can and threw up in it. "Maybe, I better get some help," she said, wiping her mouth.

Dora got dressed and I held her arm to give her balance as she walked to my car. I opened my car door for her, and she crawled in the passenger seat. As we drove to the hospital, I told her about Cindy and the bad news from the morning. "Oh, Sarah," she said.

Somehow, it was the most heartfelt response I could have imagined. Here I was helping her, but in reality, she was helping me.

As we waited in the ER together, I realized that this was the first time I had ever spent time alone with Dora. The few times I had met her in person before, Roland was with me; otherwise, she and I had primarily communicated through email or texts. Dora not only had studied everything she could about food, diet and cancer but had a spiritual understanding of life, death and cancer.

The receptionist called out Dora's name and we followed a nurse through the double doors and Dora sat down on the hospital bed. The nurse hooked her up to an IV to get some fluids into her. Even though Dora hated medicine, she took some painkillers from the nurse and the color started to come back into her face. The nurse informed us that a doctor would be in shortly and left the room.

I was sitting in the chair next to her bed when Dora asked, "How are you coping with the terrible news about Cindy?"

"Dora, I feel so helpless," I said as I started to cry. "Cindy asked me not to fly out to see her, but I think I should go anyways. I want to be there for her."

"Sarah, you need to respect her wishes. This is her journey. It's not about you; it's about her."

I looked at Dora and she reached out her hand and I held it and knew she was right. "Sarah, you have to realize that Cindy is going to go through many different emotions and it's going to be hard at times to watch her go through them. She might act differently but she will never give up hope. Hope never goes away."

I wiped the tears from my face and said, "Why does she have to die?"

"Death is beautiful, Sarah. Don't be afraid of death."

Dora stared into my eyes and said, "I've died before and I'm not afraid of death."

I knew she beat her cancer diagnosis and survived it. "But you beat cancer," I said.

"I didn't die from cancer. When I was pregnant with my daughter, I had an emergency C-section. When I was in the hospital, I got a terrible infection from the surgery and I was in a coma. At one point, I actually died for a few minutes."

My mouth was wide open, and I couldn't believe what I was hearing. She continued and said, "I saw the bright light, and there was this incredible feeling of letting go, a release of energy, it was beautiful."

"Oh Dora, of all the people in the world who could have called me today and the fact that I'm sitting here next to you listening to this, is quite amazing."

"Sarah, you are going to see your friend again, trust me. I believe in reincarnation and even if you don't believe in it, you have to know that you were meant to meet Cindy. And she was meant to meet you."

I felt an electric energy come over me, a wave of comfort. Dora reached over and put her hand on my shoulder and said, "You also have to protect yourself, Sarah. You went through a life-changing experience as well, and you have to stay healthy. Wear light clothes to reflect the negative energy. Don't absorb all the stress and sadness around you. When you want to scream, just scream. If you're too embarrassed, go into the ocean, swim underwater, and scream. Get the energy out."

I started to cry again. "How is this all possible? I hear the worst news about Cindy, and here I am, with you, in the ER."

Dora smiled and said, "We're all connected."

chapter 33

AUMAKUA

The hospital released Dora and scheduled an appointment for her with another doctor at the medical clinic the following week. She had a bacterial infection of some sort and they gave her a prescription for some antibiotics to pick up at the pharmacy. The fluids helped her, and she was already feeling better on the car ride home.

I asked her if she wanted me to take her to the drug store to pick up her medicine and she declined. She wasn't going to take the medicine and she didn't go to her follow up appointment with the doctor. Dora got back to her diet and got better on her own.

The morning after I took Dora to the hospital, I called Cindy. She answered the phone and I said, "Hi, how are you feeling today."

"I'm tired, and I want to come home."

My heart ached and I said, "I know Cindy, you'll be back on Maui in no time. Hey, you won't believe what happened to me yesterday. I had to take Dora to the hospital."

I could hear the concern in her voice, and she asked, "Is she ok? What happened? I'm sorry Sarah, I'm so out of it with all the drugs they are giving me."

"Don't worry Cindy, Dora is fine, she had a bacterial infection, that's all. But Cindy, you won't believe this. In the hospital, Dora told me a story of how she had died years ago and was brought back to life. She said that she saw the bright light and had an incredible feeling of release and that it was beautiful."

With a childlike wonder in her voice, Cindy said, "Is that so?"

"Yes, Cindy. Dora said you have nothing to fear."

I hoped Dora's story comforted her in the way it did me the night before.

When Roland got home from work that evening, we were both emotionally drained. After dinner, we sat on the couch and I turned on the television. I was flipping through the channels and Roland looked over to me and said, "Let's go to the beach."

Our monthly full moon beach nights had been interrupted over the past year and I turned off the television and said, "That's the best idea I've heard of in a long time. Let me grab a blanket and we'll go."

The moon wasn't full this particular night, but it was big and bright enough to light up the beach. We laid our blanket out on top of the sand and talked. Roland was sad about Cindy, but he was also worried about me.

There were so many questions, like how the cancer returned so quickly. We were both confused but it seemed like a moot point at this juncture. Like with Anne's death, there were no answers to these questions. It was what it was, and we had to live with it. For Roland, it was another reason to stay focused on our diet and my health.

We talked about everything: Cindy, Dora, and how crazy the past two days had been. The cool ocean breeze felt good, and as we talked, I listened to the waves hitting the beach. I took in deep breaths and let them all out slowly. I thought about how Emalia and Anne were gone, and now Cindy was going to leave me too.

I could hear Dora's voice in the back of my head. "You were meant to meet these people for a reason. We're all connected," she said over and over.

I laid my head on Roland's chest and we both stared at the ocean, when something suddenly swooped past us. "Did you see that?" Roland asked.

"Yeah, what was it?"

"An owl," he said.

All of the sudden, an image of Emalia popped into my head. Even though my rational mind didn't want to believe it, I knew Emalia was reaching out to me, letting me know that everything was going to be okay.

The next morning, I told Cindy how Emalia showed up to me as an owl at the beach. She was tired but I wanted to be the person I had been during our shared treatment. I wanted to be her positive light.

"Sarah, I'm in so much pain, and I want to close my eyes and never wake up," she said.

"I know Cindy, it's okay," I said, choking up through the tears, "It's okay."

chapter 34

ELEVEN YEARS

The next day Cindy texted me: "I'm so sick, Sarah. Don't expect much when I get home. I'm going to be on heavy painkillers; they're trying to regulate the pain. They don't think I'm going to be out of here until Sunday. I'm sure I won't be strong enough to fly, but I'm going to anyway. If I could, I'd close my eyes and go right now, honestly."

I texted back: "You have been through so much the past month and year. It's okay to close your eyes. You've been through the ringer. I don't expect anything from you and understand how painful and scary this all must be. I'm here to be your friend and to love you. You have made such an impact on Roland and me. We love you so much. There is no control in life. We would like to believe there is, but ultimately life and death happens. I want you to live free of

~ 165 ~

guilt, pain, and sadness. Strong or sick, we just want you to know that we love you. You will always be my first phone call in the morning, even if you are gone. I will always think of you and the wonderful talks we had, and how you made my soul sing. I love you and hope to see you soon."

Cindy texted back an emoji sign that had a sad face with a tear running down its cheek. It was too hard to say these things out loud and reading and writing them in a text was somehow easier. I sat in silence, and we both knew how much we meant to each other.

After wiping the tears away, I got in the car and started driving without a destination in mind. Somehow, I ended up at the cancer center. I walked in and saw Serena. She was working and was startled to see me. She excused herself from her patient, and as she walked over to me, my tears started to fall.

"Cindy is going to die," I said.

Serena's face dropped and she was in utter disbelief. She hugged me and said, "Sarah, I'm stunned and want to talk more with you. I'm so sorry but I have to get back to work. Do you think you could come back in an hour, when I'm on my lunch break?" she said.

I nodded my head and went out the double doors towards the entrance of the cancer center. Before I left the building, I passed the counselor's office. I had never gone to see her before, and thought it was more for family members, than patients. The door was open, and I peeked my head in and said, "Hello?"

The counselor got up from her chair and greeted me. She could tell that I had been crying, and she handed me a tissue and offered me a seat.

Before she could say anything, I said, "My friend just got diagnosed with terminal cancer and only has a few months to live."

She comforted me and handed me a book about how to deal with the dying process of a loved one. It had a drawing of an old sailboat out at sea on the cover. She told me about the hospital's hospice program and that I could keep the book. I gathered myself together and thanked her for her time and the information she gave me.

I waited outside the cancer clinic until Serena had her lunch break. She sent a text, asking me to meet her in the conference room. I met her in the same room where I had my first appointment with the nurse that informed me of the reactions and symptoms I would have from the chemotherapy. I remembered the nurse's comment, "expect to have symptoms from your eyes to your anus," but this time there were no giggles.

Serena was in tears when I told her, "Cindy wants to close her eyes and never wake up."

I wanted information and facts. I wanted to know what to expect when Cindy came home, so I wouldn't feel so helpless. I asked Serena, "How does this happen? She was all clear, how does the cancer come back so fast? How is she going to die?"

Serena dried her eyes, and put her hand on my arm, "Sarah, there are so many things about cancer that we still don't fully understand."

I shook my head, trying to focus, "Serena, what do I need to expect when Cindy comes home? How will she look?" What kind of drugs is she going to be on? Will she be able to eat? I need to know what to expect."

"Oh Sarah, I wish I had all the answers to your questions, but I can't really fully answer them. All I know, is that you, being there for her, is going to mean the world to her."

I hugged Serena and said, "Thank you for always being here for me."

The next day, I called Cindy, and she sounded like she was in a better mood from the day before. "Serena's parents stopped by today. They brought a wonderful gift for me. Serena's mother had a photo of all us from the hike we took, and she put it in a nice picture frame. I love her perfume; I do have to remember to find out what fragrance it is."

I was relieved to have Serena's parents there and they reported to Serena on how Cindy was doing.

"Wow, Cindy that's great. Isn't Serena the best?"

"Yes, she is truly an angel in our lives."

In the midst of all the chaos, our eleven-year anniversary rolled around. I made reservations at Mama's Fish House on the night of our anniversary, Roland and I arrived early. We sat on the beach in front of the restaurant and watched the children play in the water as the sun set over the mountains. It was dreamlike, clouds hovered over the mountains and the whole sky turned pink. It was so incredibly beautiful, I snapped a picture of the sky and clouds and sent it to Cindy. I was filled with a true sense of gratitude. Even in the darkest moments, the world and nature showed it's light and beauty.

chapter 35

HIGH AS KITES

Cindy was stubborn and determined to come back to Maui. She wasn't well enough to fly but was getting on a plane and making the six-hour flight back home anyways. I convinced her to use her miles to upgrade to first class; she was reluctant at first, but ultimately, she knew that, in her condition, it would help.

Before she came home, we had talked about her healing and getting well again. Cindy said, "I know it's going to take some time for my body to recover from the surgery. I haven't smoked any pot since I've been in the hospital but when I get back, I plan on getting very stoned. I think you need to start smoking with me."

"Cindy, you know I don't smoke pot," I said over the phone.

She pleaded and said, "Come on, don't be such a square. I really don't want to do it alone."

"Okay, Miss Peer Pressure," I said, laughing, "I will smoke pot with you."

"Have you been learning how to play cribbage?"

"Yes," I lied.

She knew I was lying and chided me, "Well, by the time I get home, kiddo, you better know how! I told you all summer, to learn."

"Okay, I will, and I'll smoke pot with you, too!"

While waiting, I did try to learn how to play cribbage by downloading an app on my iPad. It was confusing, and I tried to watch a video, but was even more confused. Fortunately, my friend knew how to play, and he offered to teach me. After about five rounds, I was starting to get the hang of it, but there were so many combinations and rules, it was difficult to keep everything straight. I learned the basics and knew enough that I would be able to play with Cindy.

I was in a state of turmoil and confusion every day while I waited for Cindy to return. It was so hard to know how she was feeling, how she was doing, and what she looked like, when we just talked over the phone.

The day Cindy came home, I planned on letting her get settled in before calling or offering to come over. It was a surprise when she called me almost as soon as she got home. She wasn't feeling well and wondered if I could bring over some beet juice and our juicer.

Everything Cindy ate in the hospital had made her violently ill and she threw up a great deal. I contacted Dora for help and advice for Cindy. She told me, that with all the painkillers Cindy was on, she would have almost no good bacteria in her body to help her eat or have bowel movements, so light soups and raw beet juice would help. I never pushed my diet on Cindy but suggested over the phone to her that the juices might help her.

Cindy needed me and I was anxious and eager to finally see my friend. I grabbed our juicer and ran like the wind to the store to pick up some beets.

When I arrived at the house, Jim told me that Cindy was resting in bed. I put the juicer on the kitchen counter and showed Jim how to use it while I made some beet juice.

I walked into the bedroom with the glass of juice and saw Cindy lying in bed. She had lost a lot of weight, her hair was thin, and she appeared to have, aged a great deal in a short period of time. She heard me come in and opened her eyes. Cindy sat up and took one look at me and said, "Look at your hair."

I always had long straight hair, but it had grown back curly after my treatment. It happened to many cancer patients who went through chemotherapy and it was referred to as, "the chemo curl."

"Hey Cindy, look at you, you are home, you made it!"

I handed her the glass and said, "Here, I made you some beet juice."

She took a sip and put the glass down on the drawer next to the bed. "Well, it doesn't taste as bad as I thought it would. I must look like shit. I'm tired and need a shower."

"You look fine, Cindy. I'm going to leave but I will come back tomorrow."

Cindy took my hand and laid her head on the pillow and said, "Next time, we'll smoke together."

I laughed, "Okay, but first things first. You have to be able to eat."

As I drove away, my feelings were strange and all mixed together. On one hand, I was elated that I could now help my friend in person. She was here, in the same time zone, and I could see her face and hug her. But I also knew that I wouldn't be able to cheer her up or keep her positive like I had before. This time was different, and I cried the whole way home.

When I went to see her the following morning, Cindy was awake and more like her old self. She had more energy, and the beet juice seemed to be helping, but she was also on heavy painkillers. Her phone was constantly ringing, as friends and neighbors heard the news of her terminal diagnosis.

Serena had left the house a week before they arrived, to give Cindy and Jim their space back. Serena gave me the number for hospice, and I passed the information on to Cindy. She called hospice to set up an appointment, and the doctor was to come by the house the following day. I sat in a chair beside her bed, and she asked me to get the pot out of her drawer.

I hadn't smoked pot for at least ten years. I never had a problem with it, but I always fell asleep after smoking it, so it was never really my thing. Cindy took a glass-smoking bowl from the drawer and started to put some weed into it. I handed her the lighter that was sitting on the drawer and she lit up the weed and inhaled. She started coughing and smoke came out of her mouth. She passed me the pot and I took the lighter and lit it up. I took a deep breath and could feel the back of my throat burn. I exhaled and started coughing.

I was stoned out of my mind after one hit. The weed gave Cindy a small appetite and she asked for a soda and some crackers. We talked about all the latest gossip: how Grace's daughter joined the high school soccer team and that Julie got a new job at a tourist boutique. It was like old times, chatting away with each other and I was glad that Cindy was back home.

After twenty minutes, Cindy got tired, and I left so she could rest, but I was high as a kite. *Okay I can do this*, I told myself as I got in my car. I lived about twenty minutes away, and I concentrated as hard as I could on getting home. I focused on driving at least the speed limit, but kept wondering, *Why is everything going so slowly?*

I decided to stay in my lane and follow the car in front of me. It was an old, beat up Chevy. The guy driving it was not wearing a shirt and his bare arm hung out the window. I noticed that everyone was passing us on the right. *Go figure*, I thought, *the guy I decided to follow is stoned too*. I knew I shouldn't have driven high, but I didn't expect to leave Cindy's house so soon. Thankfully, I made it home safe and I was so hungry that I stuffed my face with carrots and nuts. It wasn't exactly munchies material, but it was all that we had in the house. I went to my room and passed out in bed.

chapter 36

THE LAST OF THINGS

The hospice doctor and nurses came over and met with Cindy. The doctor suggested she drink protein shakes to help her get her weight back up. Cindy took one sip, and sternly said, "No, I'm not going to drink this, it tastes like cardboard."

After smoking pot, it seemed as though she got an appetite and the first real meal, she requested was a frozen cheese pizza. After she ate it, she immediately threw it up. I cautiously tried to mention healthier food items to eat but she shot me a look and I shut my mouth.

Cindy consumed all my thoughts and a dark cloud started to form around me. I was stressed out and could feel the anxiety in my body. I didn't know if it was from the pot smoking or the situation. I knew that stress triggered some diseases and I started to constantly tell myself to relax to no avail. As I sat and watched my friend slowly dying of the same cancer I survived, I felt completely helpless.

I continued to call Cindy every morning, but later than I used to, since she usually slept in. I kept busy with surfing, and it helped with all the pressure and turmoil surrounding me. Julie and Grace accompanied me, and they were good friends who listened to my thoughts and concerns. Even out on the water, Cindy remained a constant in my mind.

In the afternoons, I would go over to Cindy's house to watch movies, eat pizza, get stoned, and play cards with her. Roland and I went over to Cindy's house for dinner three or four nights a week. Sometimes, we sat at the dinner table, but more often than not, we ate on her bed, sitting next to her.

After a few weeks, Cindy started to recover from her surgery, and hospice was able to manage her pain better. The color started to come back into her face and I said, "You look elegant, like Audrey Hepburn."

"You think so? I feel like getting up and putting some makeup on."

Cindy started to move around the house more and began cleaning and putting things in order. She was eating more and drinking margaritas like she did in the past. One night, she greeted Roland and I at the door with two glasses of margaritas that Jim had made. She was dressed up and had her jewelry and makeup on and it was as though she wasn't even sick. "Hey kiddo, I'm feeling better. I even got on the spin bike for ten minutes."

"Wow, Cindy. You are feeling better," I said with a smile as I drank my margarita.

"I think I might beat this, like your friend Dora. I'm going to live another ten years."

I remembered what Dora told me in the hospital, that hope never goes away. I said, "Cindy, you still should take it easy. Give it some time."

"Okay, mom," Cindy said with a smile.

It was a great night and it was surreal to see Cindy full of energy and life after watching her lie in bed for weeks. I hoped it would last forever, but sadly, the next day, Cindy was throwing up and was back in bed.

Time passed, and each day brought uncertainty about how Cindy would be. Some days were better when she had more energy, she got dressed, and even spent time outside her room. It was heartening to see her make that effort. But there were stretches when she wouldn't get out of bed for days, lost in her own quiet struggle.

Before I knew it, Halloween came around and Julie and Harvey were planning this year's haunted house. It was so strange for me to think about the previous Halloween, and how much of a difference one year could make in people's lives. I sent Cindy pictures of the haunted house and we reminisced about the last year.

There was a tone of sadness over the phone, and we both knew she wouldn't be here for the next Halloween.

Thanks to the pain medicine, Cindy managed to throw a beach party for all of her friends. She did all the planning from her bed, on her laptop, inviting all the guests and telling everyone what they needed to bring.

The party couldn't be on Valentine's Beach, where we burned our chemo bags, because Cindy wasn't strong enough to walk down the steep cliff. A friend suggested another beach further down the road, and it turned out to be perfect. We could drive right onto the sand and set up the beach chairs and tables. Jim set up some tiki torches and hung pink ribbon decorations on the trees. We were all gathered on the beach watching the sunset and Jim started a fire.

Roland and I had often joked that Cindy's beach parties were like television commercials advertising medicine; full of retired folks acting like teenagers and having a blast. Cindy was in great spirits, and she wore her makeup, her wig, and her biggest smile. She didn't stay long, as she lacked the strength, and Jim drove her home. The party continued on and I looked up at the night sky, and I knew that this was the last beach party with Cindy. I knew it was the beginning of many "last things" and I thought about how much I was going to miss my friend.

chapter 37

SISTERS

Cindy's cousin Dee flew out to take care of her. They grew up together and were very close. There seemed to be a competitive nature to their relationship, and Dee's presence seemed to get Cindy out of bed more. If Dee said, "You shouldn't do this," Cindy being stubborn, would do it.

One day, I went over to the house and saw that a neighbor was visiting and had brought over a pizza, which Cindy hadn't touched. As soon as they left, she had me break out the pot.

Cindy and I took a few hits, and the room quickly filled with smoke. Her cousin came in and began to cough and moved her hands around, trying to wave away the smoke. She smiled and joked, "Here you guys are again, getting stoned in the middle of the afternoon."

The three of us started talking and laughing, and Dee told us the story of how she had recently gotten lost at the store without her phone. "There I was, walking aimlessly through the parking lot, like a crazy woman, looking for Cindy's car. I have to say, there sure are a lot of Toyota trucks on this island."

At that point, the pot started to kick in, and we were laughing hysterically. Cindy asked her cousin to bring her a piece of crust from the pizza sitting in the kitchen. It took a really long time. When she returned, she didn't bring the pizza crust, instead, she had taken a full slice of pizza, and wiped all the sauce and cheese off. "Well, you asked for the crust," Dee said defensively.

We burst out laughing and Cindy asked, "By the way, what the hell took you so long anyways?"

"I walked out to the kitchen and looked out the window and there was a huge rainbow. I was completely mesmerized."

We all laughed and were so stoned. I looked at her cousin and figured she must have gotten a second-hand high from our smoke. As Cindy ate her crust, I noticed Dee staring at my wedding ring tattoo. "Wow, that is such a cool idea. Is that your wedding ring?" She asked, squinting at it with her stoned eyes.

"Yes," I answered. "Unfortunately, it's from a previous marriage."

Her eyes grew huge and she gasped. Cindy and I started laughing and soon Dee joined in. Tears ran down all of our faces and we held our sides from the joke and all the laughter.

Dee and Cindy shared a special bond, it was heartwarming to watch them together. They were like sisters, so close and connected. Cindy would tell me how Dee would give her the best back massages and brush her hair. It made me think of Julie and Grace and how they had become the sisters I never had.

I had spent a few afternoons with Grace, and we talked about everything. Grace had lost her younger sister to cancer years ago and understood what I was going through. "You know, when my sister died, it was very painful to watch her suffer for so long. I miss her and think about her every day. Just the other day, when I was folding the laundry, out of the blue, I thought of her and started crying."

"Oh Grace, I'm so sorry."

"Sarah, you're such a good friend to Cindy. You should know that she is lucky to have you." It was comforting, but I really wanted to hear that my friend was going to live and that we were going to talk every morning until I was old and gray.

꘎꘎꘎

It was great getting to know Cindy's cousin, Dee. She was smart, fun, and charismatic. She read *New York Times* bestsellers, film and book reviews and was cosmopolitan.

There was a certain style about her, and she was the first person you would want to talk to at a party, just like Cindy.

Hospice continued to come out weekly, and there were many medicines and schedules to keep up with. The nurses were not on duty twenty-four hours a day, so Dee had to learn how to administer her medications, change her as she was becoming more bed ridden and to remove the gauze pads on her newly forming bed sores. Dee cooked healthy dinners, cleaned, and did laundry. She monitored Cindy's visitation schedule and kept visits short.

Dee's presence and support meant so much to Cindy during this time. It was truly beautiful to witness the way Dee cared for her. She would change Cindy's bed sheets and make them tight like a hotel bed. Cindy told her that no one had ever done that for her in her entire life. Dee made warm baths for Cindy and would put moisturizer on her dry skin and rub her with a gentle touch. I had only known Dee for a short time, but I was proud to call her my friend and Cindy was lucky to have her as a cousin and caretaker.

One night after a healthy salmon dinner that Dee cooked, we stood next to each other at the kitchen sink and started washing the dishes together. Dee looked over to me and said, "You know that Cindy worries so much about you."

"I know she does," I said.

"She loves you and Roland and you two have been through so much together."

I smiled and hugged her. She had an understanding of the relationship that Cindy and I had. Cindy and I didn't have a sisterly bond and we did not have a mother daughter bond; it was something different. Somehow, having the same cancer meant that we belonged to each other.

chapter 38

THE BOYS

We all worked together to hatch a plan to get Cindy to eat more. We started sneaking protein powder into her brownies and put vitamins in the pasta. I helped out by smoking pot with her, which fired up her appetite. Cindy loved junk food in particular while smoking, and at this point, anything she put in her mouth was a good thing. The freezer was stocked with ice cream, and we were all happy to run out whenever she got a craving for fast food.

Roland was getting worried about our diet, which was difficult since I was eating lots of pizza and drinking margaritas with Cindy almost every night. Roland would scold me not to drink every time we went over, but it was something Cindy and I did together. In a way, I needed to be numb to the situation at hand.

~ 185 ~

As Cindy's cancer progressed, my fear grew. Every time my scar tissue started to act up, or I had trouble making a bowel movement, my mind started to go to dark places. I had to constantly remind myself that I was not Cindy.

We came over with pizzas one night for dinner and Roland carried them into the kitchen. I headed straight to the bedroom. "Okay, let's do this," I said as I got out the pot.

Cindy started coughing after the hit and said, "I'm tired. You go out to the kitchen and play cards and eat."

"Are you sure you don't want any pizza?" I asked.

"No, I'm not hungry," she said, closing her eyes.

Twenty minutes later, while I was sitting in the kitchen, I got a text from Cindy: "Don't forget to turn off the oven."

I relayed the message to Jim and my phone soon beeped again, and the text read: "Can I have a piece of pizza, please?"

I smiled and I had done my job. As I ate my pizza, I thought about how Jim and Cindy had always watched over Roland and me. They had become such big parts of our lives.

When we bought our house, Jim looked over our mortgage paperwork for discrepancies. The day we moved in, they came over with a bottle of champagne and cheered as Roland picked me up and carried me through the front door of our first home.

There was the time Cindy picked Doodle up from the vet the day he got neutered. She was always there to help. I remembered the year Cindy gave me the book, *Fifty Shade of Grey,* for my birthday, not realizing what it was about. We had a long laugh over that one. All the afternoon matinee movie dates, Christmas dinners, and margaritas and being three sheets to the wind together. We had made some great memories throughout the years.

Watching Cindy slowly fade away was harder than going through chemotherapy. Whenever we talked about something in the future, Cindy would get excited, then stop herself, and say, "Well, I won't be around for that."

The reality of Cindy being gone someday filled the room like the smoke from the pot and I focused on not forgetting one moment, one laugh, and one smile.

Cindy used to be a news junkie. She would stay up late watching all the news channels and then wake up early to watch the stock market. Now, the television in her bedroom was silent and dark.

One night, she said, "Jim, I need you to come and sit by me."

Jim got up from the couch and quietly sat next to her and said, "Now what?"

"Can you read to me, dear?"

Jim got up and went to the bookcase in the den and brought back a novel. "I've got to turn on the lamp and put my reading glasses on."

He opened the book and started to read out loud. I stood outside the hallway watching the two of them in awe. I could feel him trying to imagine a life without her. This quiet time between just the two of them was a loving gift to her husband.

~~~~~

I continued to spend my afternoons getting stoned with Cindy and watching movies lying next to her in bed. We ate buttery popcorn and cookies. "Don't tell Roland," I said. It was our secret and I was happy that she was eating something.

One day, we had a turkey fry with Grace's family for Thanksgiving. We didn't eat any turkey, but Roland loved frying one. I sent Cindy a photo of Roland proudly standing over the fryer, holding a twenty-pound turkey in his hand. Cindy called me and laughed. "I have a new nickname for him. I'm going to start calling him Roland the redneck!" She said.

Cindy had her favorites and Roland was treated with more attention than the rest of us. Cindy adored Roland; after all that's how we became friends. The two of them were thick as thieves. Everyone in the house said, "Roland can do no wrong in her eyes."

Cindy was always protecting Roland and had a special place in her heart for him. I remembered one dinner years ago, listening to Roland talk to Cindy. He said,

"When I drive home from work, I start daydreaming about being a stand-up comedian. I start creating jokes and comedy routines in my head. I should start writing my jokes down when I get home."

"Really Roland? Do you feel you've missed your true calling in life?" Cindy said with a giggle.

"I do, Cindy; I think I could really do it. I might even start going to an open mic night down at the local club."

"How is anyone going to understand you with your accent?" Cindy said laughing.

"It's part of his charm," I said butting in on the conversation.

"That's it, I'm going to do it. See you think it's funny, but I will show you funny," Roland said smiling.

Cindy laughed and said, "Well, make sure and save the front row for me!"

Roland had never told anyone else, besides me, his dream of being a stand-up comedian. It was something he only shared with Cindy.

I wasn't sure how Roland was dealing with Cindy's terminal diagnosis. He was quiet about it, but there were times when he sat in her room with tears rolling down his face. He had dealt with loss like this before, when his father passed away. It had been slow and painful to watch his father die of ALS, and now, he was watching his dear friend slowly fade away as well. As hard as it was for me, it must have been just as hard for him.

chapter 39

I'm Leaving On a Jet Plane

Christmas was Cindy's favorite holiday, but a Christmas party was out of the question this year. Someone had suggested a Christmas cookie decoration gathering instead of a party. Cindy huffed and said, "That is even more work than a Christmas party. I've had many, many cookie parties and let me tell you how much work they are. You need lots and lots of cookie cutters, and you have to make batches and batches and batches of sugar cookies, plus frosting in all different colors."

"Can't we just buy pre-made sugar cookie dough and frosting from the store," I said.

Cindy said, "No, you cannot go and buy dough already made at the store. They would taste like cardboard and turn out horrible."

She started talking about butter, sugar, confectioners' sugar and all the ingredients we would need. The whole time she talked, she waved her hands around like an orchestra conductor, and I could tell she was picturing the whole party, right down to the tiniest detail.

It was settled, there was to be no cookie gathering, so I said, "Can we at least make some eggnog?"

Cindy loved homemade eggnog and it was great for her because it was chock-full-of calories. She was very skinny at this point and ate very little. Cindy gave instructions from her bed on how to make the eggnog. She started spouting off all the ingredients, from sugar, cinnamon, eggs, fresh nutmeg, and rum. With my diet, eggnog was off limits, but I happily drank it with Cindy on many afternoons. I sat next to Cindy and drank my cold eggnog, and it was damn good.

After Christmas, Roland and I were scheduled to leave for a trip to see his family in Switzerland. Most people would be excited for such a trip, but it meant time away from Cindy. There was a strong part of me that didn't want to go, because I knew Cindy could pass at any moment. But Roland had such a busy year with work, and he needed this break. Plus, we needed to visit his family and they hadn't seen us for a long time.

We were leaving in the evening, so I carefully planned out the entire day of our departure, because there was so much to be done. In the afternoon, I went over to Cindy's house and watched a movie with her.

When it was over, we smoked some pot and got stoned. I started telling her about the trip and Cindy was quiet. I knew that she was sad that we were leaving.

Her friend helped her set up Skype on her phone so we could still talk every day, but I knew it wasn't the same. My phone rang and I saw that it was Roland calling. I answered and said, "I'm at Cindy's, hanging out."

Roland sounded panicked and said, "Do you know your passport is going to expire in February?"

"Yes, I know. I'll have to get it renewed when we get back home."

"No," he said, "They won't let you into Switzerland if your passport is expiring within three months."

Panic surged through me and I jumped off the bed. "I'll be home as soon as possible."

I hung up the phone and Cindy looked confused. "I'm so sorry Cindy, I have to leave right away. I love you and will call you later."

"Okay," she said puzzled by my urgency to leave.

I gave her a hug and ran out the door. We were supposed to fly out that night, it was already two in the afternoon. *This is not how I am supposed to say goodbye to Cindy,* I thought. *Is this the last time I'll see her?*

After several hours on the phone, we learned I would have to get my passport renewed in Honolulu and fly out the next day. I had to change all of our travel arrangements and get the passport renewal paperwork in order.

We went to get my passport photos taken, and I called Cindy to tell her everything.

In her way, she of course asked, "Did you at least brush your hair for the photo?"

I laughed and said, "Come to think of it, no I did not brush my hair. I was a little too busy to think about it."

I got on the plane not knowing if I would ever see Cindy again. When we landed in Switzerland, the first thing I did, was call her, and when she answered, tears poured down my face. She was still alive.

We were staying at Roland's brothers house on our trip and I called Cindy every night while we were in Switzerland; with the twelve-hour time difference, it was morning for her on Maui.

I described all the beautiful city lights and small bakeries and shops to her. She loved Europe, and she had been planning a river cruise for the fall that they had to cancel. They were able to get a full refund, but it, broke Cindy's heart.

Jim answered one evening when I called. "Cindy had a blood clot in her lung last night," he told me. "People usually die quickly from that ninety percent of the time, but she's still here and now on oxygen. She is sleeping now, so you should try to call again later."

I was alone in our room and could hear Roland talking and laughing with his family and friends outside the door. I sat there crying, thinking, *Why am I here? I shouldn't be here. I want to be at home, with my friend.* I wiped away the tears and slowly collected myself and rejoined the group.

When I called the next day, Jim answered again, and he immediately handed the phone to Cindy. "Hey kiddo," she said.

I could hear that it was hard for her to talk and that her voice was weak. I started crying and managed to say through my tears, "You gave everyone a scare, huh?"

"Yeah," she said.

There was a different energy in her voice. After nearly dying the night before, she felt a new hope. "Sarah, I'm going to live every day to the fullest."

"Yes, every day is a blessing. Cindy we will be home in a few days. Only a few more days." I said choking up.

Once we landed in Maui, we went straight to Cindy's house. Hospice had brought in a new hospital bed that moved up and down, and the oxygen machine was loud and constantly humming. She had lost even more weight and the cancer was advancing.

She was still Cindy though: she sometimes pretended to sleep when visitors came by if she was too tired to talk to them. The minute they left, she'd shout, "Let's start the movie!"

She didn't want to smoke pot anymore, so I had to peer pressure her into it, "Look at what you've done to me," I said. "Now, *I'm* the pot head."

She looked over at me weakly, "All right," she said and took a hit of the pot for me.

chapter 40

GONE

Her cousin Dee had been back and forth from the mainland and Maui for months, and she had to go back home. It tore her up inside to leave but her family needed her. By this point, Cindy was unconscious most of the time, and there was little left we could do for her.

I offered to take Dee's place and care for Cindy. Before she left, she took the time to teach me everything I needed to know. The day before her departure, I arrived at the house at four in the morning, ready to begin. It was still dark outside and there was a stillness in the air.

Dee turned on the light to Cindy's room and she was awake. Her eyes were open, but she was very weak. Faintly, she asked, "Can I have something to drink?"

Dee said, "Yes, Cindy. I will get you some water."

Cindy looked up at Dee with the sweetest eyes. I watched as Dee lightly stroked Cindy's head. I was holding Cindy's hand and said, "Cindy, I was walking Doodle and I saw the most beautiful rainbow in the sky, and I thought of you."

Cindy looked at me and with a whisper said, "I love rainbows."

"Yes, Cindy and every time I see a rainbow, I will think of you."

Cindy coughed and she said faintly, "I'm sorry you have to take care of me."

"You would be doing the same for me, if our positions were reversed. You always took care of me when I was sick."

She looked at me with sad eyes, and I said, "I love you."

Too frail to speak, she mouthed, "I love you, too."

She looked at us staring back at her and fell back asleep.

Dee left and flew home the next day and I promised her to keep her updated on everything. I woke up at four in morning and drove to Cindy's house to take care of her. It was dark out, and I could see the moon's reflection over the ocean from the lanai. The oxygen machine hummed and as I watched Cindy sleep, I thought about my own cancer, and how our roles could have been reversed.

I thought about Anne, Emalia, and what their families must have gone through. The pain and suffering not only of the dying but the living. How beautiful it was to be able to love an individual so much and how devasting to have to say goodbye to them forever.

Hours passed and after I had my coffee, I picked up some towels from the bedroom floor. I went downstairs to the laundry room and threw the dirty items in the washing machine. There were clothes sitting in the dryer from the day before and I took them out of the machine. As I started to fold a pair of Cindy's pajamas, tears ran down my face. I looked at the pink and paisley cotton top and thought of the hours I had spent lying next to her in bed, smoking, laughing, and eating popcorn. I didn't want to forget Cindy.

I walked up the stairs with the folded laundry and Jim was sitting at the dining room table. "I'm taking these. I want these pajamas," I said trying to conceal my tears.

He looked up from the newspaper and said, "Okay."

I put the clothes on the table and ran to the bathroom and started crying again. *Why did Cindy have to die? What was I going to do without her? When will this pain go away?*

I went to the living room and the hospice book was on the table. I had read it before she came home from Seattle. I picked it up and opened it again and began reading about the signs that the end was near. It mentioned breathing patterns, body temperature, skin color change, and many other symptoms that I started to look for.

Cindy was unconscious and I sat and held her hand. It was cold and pale. I knew the end was coming soon, the cancer had taken over her body.

Later that evening, Cindy passed away. I watched as she took her last breath and I told her I loved her and that she would be in my heart forever. In that moment, I could see her spirit had left her body. The tears ran down my face and I knew she was no longer in pain; she was free from suffering.

There was a quiet peace to her, and it looked as though she was smiling. All the strain in her face disappeared and my friend was gone.

I looked at the clock on the wall and I went over to the table, picked up the piece of paper with the hospice phone number and called the nurse to give them a time of death.

I sat down and sent a text message to her family and friends that Cindy had passed. The nurse arrived shortly thereafter and turned off the loud oxygen machine. The quiet seemed so strange. I followed the nurse into the bedroom, and she instructed me that we needed to wash the body.

I took Cindy's hand and held her palm in mine. Her skin was soft and her nails beautifully manicured and I stood in silence. After everything we'd been through, this was my final act of showing Cindy how much I loved her.

I went in the closet and got the dress that Cindy had picked out to wear. I put the dress on her and placed a flower lei that her cousin had bought for her and put it around her neck.

Jim came into the room later and said, "The nurse said they are going to pick her up in the morning and take her to the mortuary."

I sat down next to Cindy and looked at her and held her hand. I whispered, "You're out of pain. I love you."

When I left that night, I took one last look at her from the bedroom window. I saw her lying there, finally at peace, after so many months in pain. A quiet calm settled over me, and I knew my life would never be the same, but that it was okay because I loved her, and she loved me.

chapter 41

A MOTHER'S LOVE

Jim had a wonderful beach celebration for Cindy, and it was a typical Cindy party. I imagined that before she died, she must have given Jim strict instructions on where, when and how to throw the party. I pictured her arms and hands waving around, describing and telling Jim what to bring and who to invite. He put together an amazing photo board with pictures of her.

It was great to see old photos of Cindy and the wonderful life she had lived. When Cindy was in her thirties, she dyed her hair blond and it was a treat to see the pictures of her when she was young and beaming full of life and health.

When the time came, everyone took out their stand-up paddleboards and surfboards. Jim had his kayak on the beach, and we went out on the water. We paddled past the waves and the current was strong. The wind was blowing, and we all had small bags of Cindy's ashes. We opened them and released the ashes into the wind and said one last goodbye to Cindy. I watched as the ashes blew away. I looked towards the shore and a group of Cindy's friends were on the beach cheering for Cindy.

When we got back to shore, we were all ready to celebrate. There was plenty of alcohol and spirits for everyone and we sat in our beach chairs, drinking the sundown, and telling stories about Cindy.

"That woman really knew how to throw a party," I said to Roland, as we watched the sky change color from the setting sun.

The house that had been busy for months with nurses, doctors, family and friends was now empty. It was just Jim.

I went up to the house to help him clean up everything, and it was odd not going directly to Cindy's bedroom. I started to vacuum the house and Jim washed the bed sheets. We moved all of the bedroom furniture back into place and Jim said, "Well, there is lots of stuff here. Take anything you want of Cindy's."

"Thanks Jim, I have a pair of her pajamas, and that's all I want," I said, as we finished moving the furniture.

We went into the kitchen and Jim took a glass out of the cabinet and went to the fridge to get me a glass of ice water. I sat at the kitchen table where Cindy used to make lunch and tea for me. I closed my eyes and imagined her standing next to the stove, laughing at a funny story I just told. She did make my heart sing and the void that was created when she left was too big for me to comprehend.

The light that lit up when she would walk in a room was dark now. The eagerness to wake up early to call her, vanished. She was a force of nature, and now, was no more.

Jim went to the recycling bin where he kept the old newspapers and brought me a paper that he had put aside for me. He said, "I read this article a few weeks ago and I remembered that you had mentioned that you knew her. She, you and Cindy all had colon cancer."

I set the paper down on the table and saw it was an interview with Emalia's mother under the title, *A Mother's Love.* She had helped her grandson deal with grief and cope with the death of his mother and wanted to help others. She had started a non-profit foundation to help and give support to children and family members who had lost loved ones. She named it after her daughter, Na Keiki O Emalia, which translated into "Emalia's Children"

I finished reading the article and it warmed my heart. I thought about Roland and the grief and struggles he went through as a child, dealing with the loss of his mother and father. The last few years, our relationship had been put through so much. Through everything, he had been my rock and loved me unconditionally.

I looked over the article once more and I could hear Dora's voice in my ear saying, "It's all connected."

chapter 42

ANGER AND ANXIETY

A week after Cindy's beach celebration, I ran into Bill at the post office. He was back from the mainland and I had known that he was coming back, but with everything going on, I had completely forgotten the dates. He had flown in two days before and was back on Maui for a few months to figure out the house situation.

I gave him a big hug in the parking lot, and I told him about Cindy. He said, "That's cancer for you. It's evil and horrible and I'm sorry about your friend."

"How have you been?" I asked.

"Well it's been over a year since Anne passed and I still can't get over it. I don't think I ever will be, to be quite honest. The girls are flying in next week and we should all get together. I can't believe it's been a year since they've seen you."

Gosh, has it already been a year since they were here? I wondered.

It was nice to see Laura and Leigh again. Laura was now a new mom and Leigh brought her daughter, who was now over a year old. I told them about Cindy, and we talked about how difficult it was to watch someone die from terminal cancer. They understood and had gone through similar things with their mother, Anne.

Loneliness and grief weren't allowed to sneak in while they were here. I stopped by their house every day and kept busy with Bill and the girls. Bill had spent the past year figuring things out, and he came to the conclusion that his life on Maui without Anne was pointless. He was going to put the house on the market, and it sold quickly. Their dream of retiring and living on Maui was over and I sadly said goodbye to my friends when they left.

Alone in my room, I would occasionally listen to old voicemails from Cindy to hear her voice. She was the closet person to me that had passed away. I lost my grandparents when I was young and remembered being sad, but I didn't really know them. Cindy was part of my daily life for years and now she was gone.

One afternoon, I was at the park and got into an argument with a neighbor. It was for something small and silly, but when I got home, I couldn't control myself and broke down crying. I missed Cindy so much. I thought about all the stories I had accumulated over the past few months; stories I would normally tell Cindy over the phone. That we would laugh about together.

Waves of sadness washed over me. I was alone. I thought about the cover of the hospice book, the lonely sailboat floating in the water. At first, I thought it represented the deceased person's soul departing into the unknown, but now I saw myself on that boat, drifting and lost.

There were times when I would get mad at Cindy for dying. I was angry with her, for not eating enough while she was alive, for not fighting hard enough. My rational mind knew it wasn't her fault, it was the cancer and I knew that she didn't want to die, but my grief blinded me. I imagined having a baseball bat and smashing everything in sight, out of pure anger. I was mad that life moves on, and that I was stuck in the same spot without my friend.

I wanted to be the person I had been the previous summer, so strong and fearless. But Cindy wasn't here, and I was struggling. The dark cloud had returned and the anxiety I had confronted was now staring me in the face. I felt guilty and tried to see the positive, but all the fears were rushing back at me.

The memories of the dead followed me around like my shadow. I took Doodle on morning walks up the street and walked past Anne and Bill's old house. When Doodle would sniff around the driveway and bushes and I wondered if Buddy's scent was still around. Standing in front of the house, I thought about the first time I met Anne. I held my hand against my chest where my port used to be.

When I took Doodle to the park in the afternoons, there were times when the clouds looked like they did when I first met Emalia. I watched the sun go over the mountains and thought of her. When I took Doodle on his nighttime potty walk, I looked up to the sky, and hoped to catch a glimpse of an owl flying by. I had nightmares of Cindy dying, and I watched her die over and over in my sleep.

One afternoon, I came home from running errands, and Doodle, excited as always, jumped on the couch to lick my face. I looked down at his stomach and noticed that it was bulging. Fear overcame me. *Does he have a tumor or something?*

I picked up the phone and called the vet. I was panicked and told the woman on the phone that my dog had a lump on his belly. The receptionist was kind and told me to bring him in and the veterinarian would see him. I put Doodle in the car, and we raced to the vet. He was in the back seat and was excited to be getting a car ride. Even though he was acting normal, I could only imagine the worst.

Doodle was my child, my companion; he was there for me whenever I needed him. When I was sick, he got me out of bed and his smile and wagging tail brought me joy every day. It crushed me to think that there was something wrong with him. *No, please don't let anything happen to him*, I thought, as I drove to the vet.

The veterinarian examined Doodle, noting that there was hardness and swelling around his penis area. My worry increased, until the vet explained nonchalantly, "Sometimes when male dogs get excited, they have swelling."

"Oh," I said, feeling slightly dumb.

Doodle had a boner.

The vet assured me that Doodle was fine, and he didn't charge me for my visit. I was humiliated. Doodle had an erection, and I thought it was a tumor. I called Grace and told her my embarrassing story, expecting her to laugh at me or think I was crazy. Instead, she said, "Sarah, you just lost someone very important to you. It's only natural to fear the worst right now."

I went home and held Doodle close. Grace was right, and I wasn't sure if I could ever be that strong person from the previous summer again.

chapter 43

THE FIN

I kept myself busy with surfing. I pushed myself to do it, even if I didn't want to. I knew if I stopped, I might never go back into to ocean.

One day, when I was out on the water paddling, and a large sea turtle surfaced for air right next to my board. I thought of Cindy. I remembered the time Roland and I had invited her and Jim to a beach near our house to watch the sea turtles exiting the water and coming up on the shore.

Around sunset, for some reason, at this particular beach, the turtles slowly made their way up onto the sand. We had brought beach chairs to watch them and Cindy was in awe. I remembered that she had said, "These creatures are magnificent. This is truly magical."

Every time I saw a sea turtle, I thought of Cindy.

One day, Julie called me and said, "Come on, let's go surf the harbor."

It was the beginning of spring, and typically the waves were smaller and scarcer but this year there were still huge north swells, like you would see in the winter, rolling in. During the summer months, we surfed the south side of the island for the more forgiving and smaller swells. The north shore waves intimidated me, even though I lived there. I had only surfed the harbor a few times and I had wiped out and ate it on the waves there. I was scared, but reminded myself, *I am strong again, I have to jump over my shadow. I can do this.*

"Alright, Julie. I will meet you there in an hour," I said and hung up the phone.

I put my bathing suit on, got my board and paddle ready and got in the car and headed towards the harbor. Julie was already there with her surfboard and rash guard on. I took the board off the roof of my car and grabbed my paddle and hopped in the water with Julie. We paddled out, and I slowly started to relax.

Julie was full of excitement, as this was one of her favorite surf spots. I tried hard not to get wet, because with all of the tankers and cruise ships that came through, the harbor water wasn't the cleanest. I caught a few waves, and my fear started to subside.

Julie had an ear-to-ear grin and said, "Isn't this so great? The sets are coming in so clean and glassy. I've already caught three waves."

"Yeah, the waves here definitely have some power to them," I said smiling back.

I looked behind me and saw a wave coming. I started to paddle for it and before I dropped in on the wave, I heard the crashing sound of the wave behind me. I thought, *Oh shit. This is gonna suck.* The wave lifted my board and I flipped right off of it. I was tumbled in the water, and as I reached the surface, I saw my board floating upside down with the fin missing. *Strange*, I thought, and another wave crashed down over my board and me. I caught my breath and frantically flipped my board over and hoisted myself back onto it.

I looked down and saw the tendons in my calf had been torn open and blood was gushing out. The cut was deep, and I could see the fatty tissue on my leg. I examined my whole body and saw that my board shorts had been sliced open too. There was another cut on my butt and on the side of my thigh. My adrenaline was racing, and it didn't occur to me to cut off the circulation with a tourniquet. Luckily, it didn't seem to cut a major artery. I realized that the fin on my board was like a sharp knife, and it had sliced open my leg and skin.

"Julie, I'm hurt! We have to get out of the water!" I yelled as I paddled as hard as I could, thinking, *Oh shit, oh shit, oh shit.*

It was about a two-minute paddle back to shore, but it felt like forever. I kept looking down and watched the blood spill out of my leg. As I got closer to shore, I spotted a surfer getting into the water and yelled for help. He paddled out to me and helped me with my board. Some more surfers that were getting ready to go out grabbed me and helped me out of the water. I couldn't put any weight on my leg, and I screamed in pain when I tried to stand.

By sheer luck, Harvey had stopped by the harbor to watch Julie and I surf. He pulled his car up next to me and offered to be my personal ambulance. The surfer that had helped me out of the water, put me in the backseat of the car. People asked around for a first aid kit and bandage to staunch the blood. A woman ran over with one, and someone else wrapped my leg with gauze. My leg was shaking in the car, and Harvey was chatting away, trying to keep me calm.

I had yet another trip to the emergency room. Harvey pulled up in front of the entrance and an orderly helped me get out of the car. He had a wheelchair for me and rolled me into the waiting room. Julie and Roland arrived soon after. I was cold and shaking and a nurse brought me over a blanket. They got me into a room quickly, and I laid there, waiting for the doctor.

When the doctor came in and asked what had happened, I informed him that I had been surfing in the harbor. The doctor shot me up with some painkillers and I screamed out in pain from the needle piercing my skin.

The diagnosis was nine stitches and that I would live. I had three stitches on the inside of my leg and six more on the outside. As I moved my leg, I could feel the pull of the stiches on my calf muscle. Harvey and Julie saw that I was okay and left. Julie had grabbed my gear from the harbor, and they would stop by our house later to drop off my board and paddle. When Roland and I were alone in the room, I started to cry, and said, "I'm sorry."

I couldn't stop crying and the tears poured out of me. Roland asked, "Are you in that much pain?"

"No, I just miss her so much."

I was crying because all I could think about was Cindy. About how she should be on the other end of the phone as I told her about yet another Sarah adventure. About how much I missed her in this emergency room I knew so well.

chapter 44

JAWS

I was not allowed to put any weight on my leg for ten days and the nurse brought me some crutches. I hated the crutches, and Doodle hated them even more. Roland had to help me with almost everything, I couldn't carry anything because of the crutches and he even had to lift me into the shower. I didn't like being helpless at home, but the time went fast, and I soon got my stitches taken out.

Grace encouraged me to get back in the water as soon as possible. She said, "When you fall off a horse, you have to get back in the saddle."

I knew she was right and went paddling with her a few days after my stitches were out. Grace kept an eye on me the whole time and said, "What a bummer about your leg, but hey it's a great day to be out on the water!"

She was so positive and patient with me. I looked at her and smiled. I had always been amazed by and envious of how calm she was on the water. Every surf session, she would paddle far out past the reef break and mediate or do yoga on her board. It was like the ocean was her second home.

After I caught a few waves, the idea of my board hitting me again didn't even faze me. It was indeed a great surf session, and I went home with a sense of certainty and pride.

There was some surf on the south side of the island and Julie, and I planned to go surfing, the following day. We drove together and Julie squealed with excitement when we passed the cliffs and saw the surf break. Julie's eyes got big and she was like a kid at a candy store. "Oh my god, look at the waves! It's going to be so much fun! Surf's up for sure," she said.

"Yup," I said. I was feeling a little nervous, but I knew it was going to be fun.

It was crowded at the surf spot we normally went to and Julie said, "Hey, look over there," and she pointed off to the right, "There is no one over at Woody's. We should go over there, we'll have all the waves to ourselves."

Every surf spot has a name, such as Pipeline, Ala Moana Bowls, Thousand Peaks, Pavilions, and so on. Woody's was one such spot. "You, sure you want to go over there? It's a far paddle," I asked.

"Yes. Come on, let's go," Julie, answered and she started paddling towards Woody's.

I followed her and when we got to the surf break, it was only the two of us. I quickly caught a nice wave and was stoked. I paddled back past the surf break to wait for the next set of waves to come in. Another stand-up paddler joined us, and two more surfers paddled out to the break.

I could see a large set of waves coming towards us and I paddled hard to get past the surf break, as everyone on the inside got swept up and thrown around by the waves. I barely made it past the waves, and I was happy that they didn't crash on top of me.

I was the only one outside the break, and as I looked down, I saw a shark bigger than my board, glide by me. It was close to the surface and it looked about fifteen feet long. Time stood still for me. The shark looked so smooth as it passed by me. I watched as it made a brushing movement with its tail through the water. Everything was dead silent in my mind.

I very slowly turned my board the opposite direction of the shark and got on my knees. I prayed that it wouldn't come back up and bump me off my board. I remained quiet and slowly put my paddle in the water, trying not to make a sound.

As I got near the surf break, the other stand-up paddler was close enough to me and I waved for him to come over to me. Trembling and still on my knees, I said, "I just saw a huge tiger shark."

"Well, let's not tempt fate. Let's get out of here." He said, clearly having heard enough. I paddled towards Julie and said, "Holy shit, Julie. A shark swam right next to me. We need to get out of the water now."

We started paddling to shore and told the other surfers we passed about the shark. It wasn't until we were halfway back that the fear and panic washed over me. My mind screamed and I thought, *Holy shit! Why is this happening to me?*

I paddled faster to get out of the water and my adrenaline was rushing. The moment I put my feet on the sand, I fell to my knees. I was safe.

A local surfer in the parking lot heard my shark story and said, "You know you don't have to get scared until the music starts."

He laughed and started singing the song from the movie Jaws. I was able to laugh because I was now safe and back on land. He said, "You're so lucky. You know not many people see sharks while surfing, and you got so close and nothing bad happened."

I was having a tough time trying to see the positive aspect out of the experience, but I said, "Yeah, right."

I thought, *I don't feel lucky. I feel like bad luck and black clouds are following me again. Why did the shark have to come right next to me? Why didn't it bother someone else? I could have stuck my hand out and touched it. Of all people, why did it have to come by me?*

I called Grace and told her about my shark encounter. She said, "Sarah, this was a random thing. Sharks live in the ocean. You don't have a black cloud following you."

"I know Grace, but why are these things happening to me? The shark, the stitches, Cindy, my cancer, it's a lot! I'm so scared and I don't want to die."

"Oh Sarah, you've had so much happen to you. We all are going to die at some point. It's part of being human. Don't try to blame or be angry, instead take all these lessons you have learned and grow from them. You are stronger than you give yourself credit for. Never forget that."

"Thanks, Grace."

"Sarah, I couldn't imagine my life without you, and I will always be here for you. Now let's get you back in the water. Are you free on Friday to go paddling?"

"Friday sounds perfect," I said.

chapter 45

LONG TIME NO SEE

I t was a dry spring, and the lack of rain had brought ants inside my kitchen. I went to the store to pick up some ant traps. As I walked through the aisles, I saw a man that looked familiar. As I got closer, I recognized him and called out, "Hi, Mikey!"

I was elated, the last time I had seen him was at the cancer center when we were getting our chemotherapy together. He put down the item he was looking at and said, "Hey, look at you! Long time no, see. You've filled out and got some muscle now."

"You too! You look great!" I said.

He gave me a hug. I couldn't get over how happy I was to see him. "Geez, the last time I saw you, you looked pretty sick," I said.

"Yeah, it was tough, and the radiation was even tougher. But once it was over, I got better and got back to work. I'm in remission now, and just living life."

"I'm in remission too," I said, smiling back at him.

"I've got to get back to shopping, but good to see you and stay healthy."

"You too, Mikey, I guess I'll be seeing you around!"

I left the store happy, knowing that he was okay.

chapter 46

LETTING GO

Time had passed, months went by and life went on. My biggest fear was forgetting Cindy. I didn't want to let go of the details and little quirks that made her so special. A friend suggested that I write a list of "Cindy-isms down so I could reminisce and remember. Julie and Grace continued to go surfing with me to help me heal. Roland suggested that I see a counselor to help me deal with my anger and grief and I started going to therapy. Everything helped but there was a void in my heart and soul.

I came home one afternoon, and my muscles were stiff. There was an underlying anger inside, seeping through me. I knew it was because of Cindy. I took my phone out of my pocket and wanted to talk to someone.

~ 221 ~

I looked at my favorites list and Roland's name appeared on the top of the list. I knew he was working, and we would have only talked about what time he is coming home and what we should eat for dinner. I saw Cindy's name on the bottom of the list. I never moved or deleted it and I kept it there because I needed her to still be alive.

I knew deep down inside who I needed to talk to. I went to my contact list and typed in Dora's name.

I called her and when she answered, her perky tone cheered me up instantly. "Hi Sarah, I was just thinking about you!"

"Hi Dora, sorry it's been so long."

"Don't worry about that Sarah. I've been keeping myself busy. I've been in Idaho for the last few weeks, helping my daughter. It's been snowing like crazy. How have you been doing?"

I broke down and started to cry. "Dora, I'm so mad inside, I can't help it, I've been angry all week. I get so mad that Cindy died. I don't know why; I know it's stupid to feel this way."

With compassion in her voice she said, "Oh, Sarah please don't be so hard on yourself. Listen people get angry when they lose their purse, their wedding ring, something that can be replaced! You lost your friend; you have every right to be angry."

"It's hard Dora, having all these feelings. Grief and sadness overcome me at times, and I can get so mad at Cindy sometimes."

"Sarah, you need to forgive Cindy and learn to let her go. When my best friend died of cancer years ago, I missed her so much that my heart ached. Cindy loved you and she taught you about friendship and life. Remember the good times and know that she is always going to be with you."

"I know Dora, you're right. I've been holding onto this anger for so long."

"It's part of the grieving process, my dear. Think about how scared she must have been, knowing that her time on earth was ending. It could have been so lonely for her, but she had you and the people she loved around her. You were a gift to Cindy."

The tears were running down my face and I said, "I miss her so much. I feel so powerless and weak at times."

"Sarah, you are brave and strong. Now, listen to me, when you get in a funky mood, I want you to wear the color red. Do you have red underwear? I want you to wear them underneath your clothes, like superman."

"Dora, stop you're making me laugh."

"I'm serious Sarah, wearing bold and bright colors, will make you feel like a superhero, untouchable, and in control."

I wiped away the tears on my face. Dora's loving voice and advice helped; the stiffness and anger began to fade from my body. Dora continued, "Sarah, you have been so blessed. You could have died when you were a baby abandoned in front of the restaurant. You could have died from cancer. But you didn't. You have your family and your friend's love and support. Never forget how blessed you are."

"Thank you, Dora for always being there for me."

I hung up the phone and I closed my eyes. I was alone in my room and it was quiet. Dora's words calmed me. I felt at peace and knew I was starting to heal.

chapter 47

HONEYMOON

It was the beginning of September and I hadn't left the island since our last trip to Switzerland. The thought of travelling scared me, and I was in my comfort zone at home, where I felt safe. I was still surfing but I couldn't push myself to do or try new things.

My fear paralyzed me at times. The smallest things started to scare me. If my car made a funny noise, I felt anxious and imagined being alone with my car broken down on the side of the road. I had flashbacks of Cindy's bedsores and lifeless body and would cry in the shower; afraid I was going to die.

I knew I had insecurities from being teased as a child and the feelings of being the last person chosen for the kickball team, or never being invited to a slumber party, showed up like a bad pimple. It felt like I was being picked on and that if something bad was going to happen, it was going to happen to me. My therapist told me I had post-traumatic stress disorder and symptoms of depression.

I worked every day on getting better and knew I had the strength and courage to overcome my fears. One evening, Roland came home from work and while we were sitting at the dinner table he asked, "So, where do you think we should go on our vacation this year?"

"I don't want to go anywhere," I said.

"Why not? I worked all year long and haven't had a break. I think it would be good for you, and for the both of us, to go somewhere."

"What if something happens? What if I get horribly sick and we don't know where the hospital is? Or what if something happens on the plane? Or what if something happened to you and we got lost from each other?"

"Sarah, calm down," he said reassuringly, "We don't want to live in fear anymore, remember?"

"I'm sorry. I know you're right. It's like a block in my head sometimes, I feel like I can't move forward."

"We've been through some shitty things, and I know it takes time but going somewhere will be fun," he smiled and continued, "You're my favorite person to travel with, you're my favorite person in general. I'm not going anywhere without you. I'm going to be with you the whole time."

I looked at him and wanted to be strong for him. "Okay, I will look at some places tomorrow and think about it."

He pulled my chair up to him and put his forehead against mine and said, "I love you, and we are going to have a great time no matter where we end up going."

The last few years were not easy and there were times when I closed myself off emotionally to him. The stress of having cancer and dealing with Cindy's death took a toll on the both of us.

I thought about everything we had been through and how our relationship was stronger than ever. Roland, who barely spoke any English when we first met, now could move mountains with his words. We created a wonderful life together, full of love and respect.

The next day, I thought about safe places for travel and booked our flight to New Zealand. We spent two weeks travelling around the country and it was like the honeymoon we never had.

c h a p t e r   4 8

42

The afternoon traffic on the highway was moving very slowly. I stared at the car in front of me and realized how quickly the time had flown by. It had been two years to the day since Cindy died. I gripped the steering wheel tightly and thought to myself, *"It's gone, the magic has left, and my memory of her is fading."*

I knew it was foolish of me to imagine something special would happen because it was the anniversary of her death. I desperately wanted a sign of anything to make me believe again. I closed my eyes and opened them and sighed. The reality was, it was just another day and, as usual, I was stuck in traffic on my way home.

Crawling at an ant-like pace, a beat up, old, brown van began to pull out in front of me. It looked like it had been around since the 1980s and I was amazed that it was still running. I noticed right away that it was definitely not the original color. It had been spray painted a dirt color brown from top to bottom. A rainbow was painted on the side of the van and there were cliché, "Peace, Love, and Happiness" sayings strewn everywhere at random on the van. I chuckled and thought, *hippies gotta love them.*

As it finished pulling out, I started to see the back of the van. It was staring me right in the face. I let go of the steering wheel and let out a deep breath. *Really? Really?* I was almost laughing out loud at the absurdity of it all. I never imagined this to be the sign but there it was on the back of an old rusted out piece of junk.

On the back of the van, was a drawing of an owl covering the whole back end. It looked like the cartoon character from the lollipop commercial. I asked myself, *"Is this really a sign?"*

I knew it was, and an image of Emalia emerged in my mind. I smiled the rest of the drive home.

My next six-month checkup with the oncologist was coming up and I had to get my blood work done a week before my scheduled appointment. I went to the clinic and I sat down on a hard-plastic chair and waited. The nurse called my name and I was directed to go into a small room. I sat down and stared at the wall in front of me. I clenched my right hand tight, and I started to rapidly open and close my fist to get my blood flowing.

There were medical posters, held up by tape, hanging on the wall. I thought about the side effects caused by having blood taken. I read that some people experienced dizziness, lightheadedness, or possibly fainted. People were advised to stay hydrated and to keep a bandage on the site where the needle went in. I remembered passing blood donation centers in school and the donors walked away with a sticker and a big cookie in their hands.

A middle-aged technician entered the room wearing all blue and went straight for the cabinet. She huffed and said, "People are always moving things around and I can never find what I'm looking for."

After opening a few drawers, she found what she needed. She took out some rubber gloves and needles. She started to put the gloves on, and a cowardly laugh came out of me when I saw the needles. I said, "I have small veins."

Doubtful, she looked at me like; *Really? I'll be the judge of that.* I repeated, "I really have small veins, every time I get blood drawn, they have to get the special needle."

She seemed to ignore me and turned around on her swiveled chair. She grabbed the paperwork from the desk and proceeded to go through the routine I knew so well. Looking at the paper she asked, "Name?"

I answered, "Sarah Sprecher."

She read aloud my date of birth and asked, "Is this correct?"

"Yes," I said.

A smile came across her face and she said, "Hey, it's your birthday today!"

Like I didn't know, I thought to myself.

It was Monday morning and it was the only day off I had that week. I was now 42 years old and the age brought up many emotions for me. Emalia had died when she 42 years old.

The nurse asked, "So, what are you going to do on your special day?"

I looked up at her and joked, "You're looking at it."

I thought about the birthday parties I had when Cindy was alive. I remembered the birthday card she had given me that read, "*We'll be friends forever. Maybe even longer,*" and it made me think about when she purchased the card. I imagined she bought it before she was sick and got the card because she was worried that I might die. I thought, *She always knew the truth, that we would be friends forever and for even longer.*

The nurse brought out the antiseptic wipes and she rubbed one over my open forearm and I tried to flex a little. My fist was still clenched. She said, "You don't have to make a fist anymore."

I knew this, but it was ingrained in me to hold my fist as tight as I could. She wrapped the rubber strap around my bicep, and I looked away. I didn't like seeing the needle or the plastic capsules that held my blood.

In her most calming voice, the nurse said, "Okay you're going to feel a pinch and now try and take a deep breath."

The prick of the needle made me cringe. I closed my eyes and remembered Cindy joking about her large veins. I knew Cindy would never have to feel the pain of the needle or have her blood drawn again. We had the same cancer, but she was dead. Sitting with my eyes closed, I finally stopped making a fist and relaxed my hand. I knew how lucky I was to be alive.

chapter 49

HOKULE'A

Serena called me one evening and invited me out for one last fun girls' night. She was getting ready to move back to the mainland and she wanted to spend some time with me before she left. For our girls' night out, Serena had booked a stargazing cruise on a boat that departed from the town of Lahaina. It was located on the west side of the island.

We met in town and drove to the boat harbor together. There was a storm coming and Serena was worried that it might be too cloudy to see the stars. When we arrived, it was as if by magic, that the clouds vanished, and the stars filled the night sky. It was the perfect night for a stargazing cruise.

When we boarded the boat, I bumped into an old acquaintance. He said, "Hi Sarah. Wow, it's been years. I'm married now. Let me introduce you to my wife, Helen."

I gave her a polite hug and said, "Nice to meet you. This is Serena, my nurse."

Serena shook her hand and said, "I've been looking forward to this all week. I've heard amazing things about this tour."

Onboard, we went our separate ways and Serena located a spot on the upper deck towards the back of the boat for us to sit.

I felt bad and said, "I'm sorry, I know I should introduce you as my friend, but I always call you my nurse."

Serena grabbed my hand, "Darling, I'm proud to be both."

The boat moved past the harbor and we were headed west, moving toward the island of Lanai. In the wintertime, it was a popular area to watch the humpback whales. From December through April the whales migrated down from Alaska to mate and to give birth in the warm waters off of Hawaii. It was summer and the whales were back in Alaska and we were in search of stars.

I looked at Serena and I loved my nurse, who had taken care of me and who had become my friend. Serena, with her long feather earrings and glitter eye shadow on. I remembered after Cindy died, she gave me a gift. It was a rock that had the word, "STRENGTH," engraved on it. She gave it to me and said, "Sarah, I want you to hold onto this when you feel weak or sad."

I thought about how strong Serena had been, not only for me, but also for all of her patients at the cancer clinic. I once asked her how many of her patients died, and all she said was, "Too many." It was difficult for me to process that Serena had to endure so much death and loss.

She looked over to me and said, "So Sarah, how have you been doing? How are you coping with Cindy's death?"

After all the time that had passed, Serena always asked how I felt about Cindy. She understood that the grieving process took a long time. "I'm doing great, health wise. No signs of cancer."

"That's terrific news."

"I still think of Cindy every day. I actually had a vivid dream of her the other night. I dreamt that she faked her death and we secretly met up. We talked so much, and I didn't want it to end. I was sad to wake up and realize it was just a dream. I'm doing much better though. I try to only focus on happy memories of Cindy. Thank you for always asking. I really appreciate it."

"I'm happy to hear you are doing better, Sarah. You've come a long way in your journey, and we all grieve in our own time. And are you and Roland still going up to the house and seeing Jim?"

"Yes, still having dinners with Jim and playing cards," I said laughing.

"He is lucky to have you guys watching over him."

"Thanks, Serena."

A waitress came by the table and took our drink orders. When she left, I said, "Wow, Serena, I can't believe you're leaving in a few weeks. I know it's the right decision and I'm happy for you, but there is a part of me that is going to miss you so much. You're my security blanket and you're leaving."

Tears started to form from both of us.

"Sarah, I'm scared to leave Maui too. I can't believe it's been over four years since we first met. I know there are more opportunities for my reiki and the mainland has some amazing cancer centers that encompass the whole body."

I wiped my cheek and said, "It's like what Roland always said about you. You were meant to fly."

The tour was about to begin. A world-renowned astronomer narrated it: "The night sky has whispered countless stories from the beginning of time. The ancient Greeks created the constellations, linking the stars together to tell their tales."

As I looked up at the sky, she pointed out Orion's Belt and the Big Dipper. Serena squeezed my hand in excitement. The astronomer asked, "Do any of you know the star the Polynesians used to navigate with?"

Someone in the audience spoke out and said, "The Hokule'a"

Over the speakers we could hear the astronomer, "Yes, you're absolutely correct. If you look towards the Big Dipper and follow the handle, you will see a gap, and the star next to it is called the Hokule'a. The Greek's called it, Arcturus. The Polynesians didn't speak Greek and had their own names for the constellations. Every culture had its own definition and language for the stars, so feel free to connect the stars and make up your own constellations and names!"

I said, "See, Serena, even though you are leaving Maui, we will always be connected just like the stars."

The tour continued and I asked Serena what she was planning on doing for her last few weeks on Maui.

She said, "I'm trying to squeeze in everything. I went on a cocktail snorkel cruise last week and oh my god, girl! Look at these photos!"

Serena grabbed her phone and flipped through the photos and there she was in a mermaid suit sprawled out on the beach. "I found this company and they teach you how to be a mermaid. It was flipping fantastic!"

I looked at the photos of her and said, "That is so cool."

I flipped through a couple more photos and smiled. I pointed upwards and said, "Hey look, I see a mermaid in the sky right now."

Serena looked up and we envisioned a mermaid floating in the sky together. I felt the breeze on my face, and I leaned back, looking up toward the night sky. I thought of Roland, Dora, Serena, Emalia, Anne, Cindy, and all of the people who helped me through my cancer journey. How could I feel lonely or scared with so much love around me? I saw everyone I loved connected in the star-filled sky. I made up my own constellation that night and I named it, The Mermaid League.

ACKNOWLEDGMENTS

This story has gone through many stages. I originally wrote it to remember my friend that died. But in writing, it became so much more. It helped me to process my depression and grief.

And most importantly, I was able to discover that I was the hero of my own story.

I am deeply grateful to Emalia, Anne, and Cindy, whose strength and spirit during their own battle with cancer gave me courage during mine. I share their stories here with love, respect, and lasting gratitude.

I didn't do it alone. There are so many people that helped me over the years with this project. They gave me the love and support to bring it to completion.

Thank you to all the stars that helped me see the mermaid in the night sky.

Sarah Sprecher

THE MERMAID league

www.mermaid-league.com